Bumpers
&
Bed Blocks

Clive Ward

Copyright © 2017 Clive Ward/oneroofpublications.com

All rights reserved.

ISBN:10: 1546329048
ISBN-13:978-1546329046

DEDICATION

This book is dedicated to all my former army colleagues. Thanks for the memories.

ALSO BY CLIVE WARD

The Goat Killer

The Unnamed Soldiers

Army Barmy

Drill Pig & Pongo

Sir Yes Sir

If Babies Could Talk

You Wouldn't Belize it

CLIVE WARD with ELAINE WARD

Half Day Closing

In Sympathy

ACKNOWLEDGMENTS

I would like to thank my editor Antonella Caputo for her help and advice. I would also like to thank my wife Elaine for her support

FOREWORD

With this book, I've tried to bring a bit of my time in the army in the late1970's, back to life.

My journey begins with a KAPE tour of the Midlands. It goes on with the daily routine of barrack room life in Colchester Garrison and on exercise in Soltau, Germany, as air portable battalion. It ends with a trip to Hamburg's red light district, The Reeperbahn.

To tell my story, I've used a handful of fictional characters, portraying a number of different army types, from the disgusting, to the delicate, from the old sweat, to the new boy.

Using real names wasn't an option. With too many characters flying around, it would have made the book too confusing. Also, when you read through the book, you'll understand why I haven't used real names.

Forgive me if some of the content is not exactly accurate. My memory is starting to fade now. It was a long time ago. Some stories you never forget, and we've all got them.

The main storyline, may seem a bit far fetched and

shocking, or too stupid to have happened. I can assure my readers that most of it did. **Apart from a few urban myths, jokes, a bit of fiction and the odd exaggerated bullshit along the way, I think I've just about covered most things.**

I believe that we all, have, to, record our memories for future generations to look back on and, for those like me, who are museum relics. I hope it brings back your memories as you read this book.
  Good, funny or bad, here are my memories. I hope I've dug up some of yours. I wonder what they'll think in a hundred years' time.
.

In case you're not familiar with military life and have a problem understanding all the army/military slang, you'll find a useful glossary at the back of the book.
Well, here goes.

Warning!

If you have never been in the military, all you are about to read is either completely true or utter bollocks. It probably did happen, but wasn't recorded. I'll let you decide. If easily offended, I really do advise you not to read on.

.

The Characters

Private Watkinson, nickname Wocko, thicker than a Sperm whale omelette. A walking germ factory. Definitely, not first in the queue for the showers, or when the bars of soap were handed out. Oh well, he's somebody's son, but definitely, should have been shot at birth.

Private Graham Day, nickname Doris, a bit of a wimp, scared of his own shadow. He's so far up the Platoon Commander's arse, his feet don't touch the ground. He's the platoon weak link. Every platoon had one of them, but somehow, they'd nearly always end up with egg on their face.

Private Eddie Edwards, aged 32, is the old soldier of the platoon. He's been in the army for a good few years, in fact too long. He's not interested in promotion. He's what you call **Non-Tac**. He knows how to twist people round his little finger; he's an expert at shit stirring and winding people up. A good mate to have on your side, when the shit hits the fan, and it generally does when Eddie's around.

Private Colin Dobson, nickname Dobbo or Doubles. His sole aim in life is to make as much money as he can. If you borrow anything from him, it is always doubles back.

Cpl Lee Clark, nickname Clarkey and he's way out of his depth. He might be a Corporal, but he can't handle the pressure, or his men, most of the time. A bit of a loner, worries too much, moans a lot, and spends his whole army career trying to stop Eddie getting the better of him.

The Platoon Sergeant Bob Billings, nickname Beano. He hates everything, typical drill Sergeant type. Always spitting out his drill sergeant lingo. He wants to become an RSM one day, but he never will be. Doesn't trust his men, his wife, even his dog. The Platoon Commander and the Platoon Sergeant couldn't be further apart.

The Platoon Commander, 2nd Lieutenant Robert Rupert Smith. Tall, good looking, he is a mummy's boy, only just got through Officer training at Sandhurst. In my opinion definitely too soft to be an officer. He thinks all his men should be wrapped in cotton wool, much to the Platoon Sergeant's distaste, and he is very gullible. He also has a big problem pronouncing his R's.

Chapter 1

The army needs new recruits and as with any organization, needs to be promoted to the public.

![KAPE TOUR - Wardi 2017]

During the summer months, the Army sets up KAPE tours. They, involve setting up promotional stands in towns, visiting schools across the county, to engage and show the general, public, and those who are crazy enough to think about joining up, what the army/military is all about.

In 1976, our platoon was temporarily based in Bulwell Barracks, Nottinghamshire. We were just coming to the end of a three week KAPE Tour. "The army is coming to your town" said the posters. The town we were in that day was Derby. We'd set up on the town marketplace. Derby has since gained *city* status.

Private Edwards, Eddie, and Private Day, Doris, were, in charge of a presentation stand, displaying the different radio's the army were using back in the 1970's. Since the 60's, the Larkspur, was the combat net radio system used by the British Army, which was replaced by The Clansman system in the late 1970's.

'Eh Eddie, do you know anything about these radio's?' Doris asked, looking puzzled.

'Apart from switching them on, I haven't got a fucking clue. Useless pieces of junk, you can't even get radio Caroline on the bloody things, not like the old Larkspur. I don't know why they're changing them, apart from the fact they didn't work half the time.'

'But we're supposed to know all about them, it's our job,' Doris said sounding anxious.

'Well, they should have sent a signaller then, shouldn't they,' Eddie replied.

Radio Caroline

I spent many nights, listening to the in and out intermittent broadcasts of Radio Caroline and Radio Luxemburg after a night on the piss, then waking up in the morning to find it was still broadcasting. I'm sure I wasn't on my own.

Founded in 1964 Radio Caroline was a pirate radio station, broadcasting from International waters, using five different ships from 1964 to 1990.

In early 1964, Ronan O'Rahilly bought The Fredericia, a former passenger ferry, which was converted into a radio ship. He re-named the ship MV Caroline, after Caroline Kennedy, daughter of U.S. President John F. Kennedy.

The ship anchored off Felixstowe, where it began a test transmission on Friday, 27 March 1964. On Saturday, 28 March the first programme was broadcast. Presenters Tony Blackburn, Johnnie Walker, Dave Lee Travis, Tommy Vance and other household favourites regularly recorded for Radio Caroline.

Suddenly, a young spotty faced, male army cadet, dressed in uniform, approached the stand. He was staring intently at the radio.

'Excuse me mate, is that the new UK PRC 352? I think you'll find the radio isn't correctly assembled, and I'm sure that's the wrong antenna you're trying to put on it and... blah... blah.'

Eddie and Doris looked at each other in confusion.

'Fuck off you little toe rag, or I'll shove this ant... anten... aerial up your arse,' Eddie said, through gritted teeth, as he pointed the aerial at the cadet.

Eddie and Doris watched, as the kid scurried off towards where our Platoon Commander was standing.

'Shit! We're in trouble now Eddie.'

'That told him didn't it, Doris? Cheeky little shit... trying to tell us how to put a radio together... for crying out loud we're professional soldiers.'

'But Eddie, cadets look up to us regulars as virtual gods, you 've probably scared him off for life.'

They watched as the Platoon Commander headed in their direction. He didn't look happy.

'I saw that. What on earth were you doing with that wadio awial Edwards?' he asked, as he reached the display stand.

'The kid was being cheeky sir.'

'Edwards, you can't go awound wacking potential wecruits with wadio awieals.'

'It's ok sir, the aerial isn't damaged.'

At the same time, me and Doubles, the latest member of the platoon, were busy on our stand, showing off some of the personal weaponry, the SMG, SLR and the section machine gun, the good old GPMG, when two good looking young girls approached our stand.

'Wow! Which one of you boys has got the biggest weapon, then? Would you like us to unload it for you?' they said, giggling away to each other.

'Looks like we're in here Doubles,' I said.

I spoke too soon. Corporal Clarke and Sergeant Billings chose that moment to come and rescue us.

'Right. You two, piss-off on your dinner break. Me and Corporal Clarke will take over. Make sure you're back here for 1300 hours.'

'But...'

'But... what? Bugger off! Be back in one hour. OFF YOU GO!' said Sergeant Billings.

'Right ladies, where were we?' I heard Billings say, as we walked away from the stand.

'Talk about pulling rank,' Doubles moaned.

'I wouldn't worry about it Doubles, once Clarkey starts chatting bollocks. Those girls won't be hanging around for long. You can be sure of that,' I said.

As we glanced back at the display stand, Clarkey, was in full flow, reeling off every fact he knew about the weapons on display.

'So, ladies the L1A1SLR, self-loading rifle, designed 1947 to 1953 range 600 metres, muzzle velocity 823 metres per second, weight... 5.7 Kg empty, capable of firing 40 rounds per minute...'

The girls didn't look impressed. Those weren't the kind of weapons they were looking for.

'Well, you fucked that up didn't you Clarkey. Look

what you've done, they're walking away,' Sergeant Billings said, as the girls disappeared into the crowd.

Armed Robbery

We made our way through town, carrying our SMG's slung over our shoulder, something that would never happen today.

'Lunch is on you Wardi,' Doubles said.

'I'm skint mate. I need to go to the bank.'

'Me too. I know, we'll go to the bank and get £10 out on our ID cards,' Doubles suggested.

Back in the 70's, for a member of the armed forces, it was possible to withdraw a maximum of £10 over the counter from their bank account, using their ID card as proof of identity. So off we went to the bank to do just that, but we didn't expect the reaction we got when we entered the bank.

Most of the bank staff dived behind the counter.

Maybe it was something to do with us still carrying our personal weapons. They must have thought it was a bank raid or something. Then the bank manager appeared to reassure the staff.

'It's ok everyone. They are just part of the army display team from the marketplace across the road.'

'Yes, gentlemen, what can I do for you?' asked the teller.

'I'd like to withdraw £10 using my ID card, please,' I said, giving the pretty female teller my details.

After a while, she came back to her desk. 'I'm sorry, sir. We're having problems finding your bank account,' she said, looking apologetic.

'What, are you sure? I've done this dozens of times, and never had this problem before,' I replied, with my right hand tightly gripping my shouldered SMG. I think I was stressing her out. I started to get more and more pissed off.

'Can you check again please,' I said

She checked again and again and still couldn't find my details.

'I'm sorry sir, I don't know what to say. Are you sure you're with this bank sir?'

'Of, course I'm with this bank. I've been with Nat West since I joined the army,' I answered, feeling really pissed off.

'This is Barclays bank sir,' she said, with a sarcastic smile on her face.

I was left red faced and speechless, Doubles just stood there laughing. I made a quick exit from the bank.

Expert in Guerrilla, Warfare me

Back at the Marketplace, it was one of the hottest days of the year and Wocko was dressed in full sniper gear. Basically, walking around looking like a large fucking bush, he stood out like a sore thumb.

'Are you ok in there pwivate Watkinson?' the Platoon Commander asked, 'Watkinson can you hear me?' he persisted.

The Platoon Commander turned to Sergeant Billings looking confused.

'Sergeant Billings, Pwivate Watkinson doesn't seem to be attwacting any potential wecruits.'

'That's not Watkinson sir, that's actually a bush.

Watkinson is over there, I can smell him,' Sergeant Billings answered.

'So, it is Sergeant Billings,' the PC said, as he put on his glasses.

The PC and Sergeant Billings looked on in amazement as a large group of young girls surrounded Wocko.

'It looks like he's attwacted a bit of a gathewing, well done that man. I wonder what he's talking to them about.'

'Oh God, he isn't exposing himself again, is he?' whispered Sergeant Billings.

Moving closer, Sergeant Billings and the Platoon Commander just caught the tail end of what Wocko was saying.

'So, there I was, alone in the jungle, but I wasn't worried, I'm an expert in guerrilla warfare me, and with guns and knives, trained to live off the land... Those long lonely nights with no female company...'

'Watkinson get over here, NOW!' Sergeant Billings shouted, in his best parade ground voice. 'Everyone else start packing away, it's an early finish today.'

'You wanted to see me Sergeant,' Wocko said.

'Yes Watkinson. The PC seems to think you have good interpersonal skills, and would make an excellent recruiter. Personally, if I was to hazard a guess, I would say you were filling their heads full of bullshit and corrupting their tiny little minds.'

'No Sergeant, I was doing my job.'

'Anyway, it's your lucky day Watkinson. The PC, God only knows why, wants me to reward you. Is it you who had a granddad who fought in the Second World War?'

'That's right, Sergeant. I've got a picture of him, would you like to see it?'

'Put it away Watkinson. I can't fucking believe that your granddad fought for this country to save the likes of you! What on earth was he thinking? Listen up, you and one other, I'll let you choose who, as long, as it's not Edwards, will report to the local British Legion tonight at 1930 hours. Transport provided.'

'What for Sergeant?'

'To play fucking table tennis! ...I don't fucking know, ask the PC, just be at the guard room at 1900 hours!'

Wocko plus one, were in for a good night. They were to be guests of the British Legion, a great honour.

Which usually meant a never ending, supply of free beer, until the early hours if you lasted that long. All they had to do was sit and listen to a never, ending conveyor belt of war stories.

Chapter 2

The British Legion

Back at camp, everyone wanted to be Wocko's plus one, for a night of free beer.

'Come on Wocko, take me, my granddad was a First World War hero,' Doris said.

'Was he?'

'Yes, his job was to stop the enemy from getting their secret messages,' Doris answered.

'He ate the fucking carrier-pigeons, didn't he Doris? 'Eddie commented sarcastically.

'Very funny,' Doris replied.

'Take me Wocko,' Eddie said, 'my granddad survived the whole war.'

'Wow, was he a hero then Eddie?' Wocko asked.

'Not really. He spent the whole war locked up as a conscientious objector.'

'Sorry Eddie, Sergeant Billings said not to pick you, you've been ruled out.'

'I know why that is,' Clakey added. 'He got invited to one of them British Legion do's a few years back, didn't you Eddie. After getting totally rat arsed, he climbed up on a row of tables, pulled his trousers down, stuck a rolled up, newspaper up his arse and lit it up like a torch. He then ran up and down the tables performing a dance called, "the dance of the flaming arseholes." Isn't that right Eddie?'

'They loved it! My dad told me the dance used to be

performed regularly by the troops in the desert during the war. Those old timers lapped it up,' Eddie replied.

'But unfortunately, their wives didn't, and word got back to our CO, who went fucking ape shit,' Clarkey answered.

'Only because he missed it,' Eddie said

'What about you Wardi?' Wocko asked.

'My granddad Jack was in the Second World War, he was a dispatch rider with the Royal Signals, got shot several times,' I replied.

'Right, that's it. I've made my choice, it's you Wardi. You're coming with me. Hurry up and get ready, the transport leaves in 10 minutes.'

The rest of the lads in the platoon were a little pissed off that I was chosen, but Wocko had made his mind up. Off we went, dressed in smart casuals, both looking forward to a never ending, supply of free beer.

The evening didn't quite go how I expected, though, and it wasn't due to a rolled up, newspaper. This was something entirely different.

Picture the scene. There we were, sat at a table surrounded by all these military vets from both world wars and various campaigns. They all wore blazers, with their regimental badges sewn onto the top pocket. This was going to be the ultimate pull up a sandbag session to end all pull up a sandbag sessions. A unique brotherhood allowing us to listen in on stories that their wives and own children have probably never heard and never will. But we could listen to these guys all night and their amazing stories of bravery, courage and self-sacrifice, as long, as the beer was flowing. And flowing, it was. The night was going really, well. The beers just kept coming. Then one of the old boys started to ask us questions.

'So, lads, did any of your loved ones serve in the military?' one old timer asked.

'Yes,' I said, 'my grandfather.'

'Oh yeah, let's hear it then, what mob was he in?' asked this ex Sergeant Major.

'He served with the Royal Signals, as a dispatch rider, he was shot several times in the back, in the final push,' I replied full of pride.

> **Dispatch Riders & Message Delivery**
>
> **The British military dispatch riders, used Triumph, Norton, BSA, and two other makes of motorbikes, during WW2. Although radio communications had improved since WW1, vast numbers of motorbikes were produced.**
>
> **Carrier pigeons were also used in WW2, the most well, known being Commando, who was awarded a Dickin medal for the successful delivery of messages from agents in Occupied France in 1942.**

'Was he really? The dirty German bastards,' one of the veterans said.

'That's typical of them lot, shooting a man in the back,' said another

'But he lived to tell the tale,' I replied.

'You must be very proud of him,' said the ex-Sergeant Major, as another beer was placed in front me.

With more drinks on the way, he then turned to Wocko, who was busy downing as many pints as he could.

'And what about you, young man, what mob was your old man or granddad in?'

'My granddad was an officer,' Wocko replied, in a voice filled with pride.

I sat there, gobsmacked. Bloody hell, you learn something new every day. Wocko's granddad was an army officer, I thought, as he pulled out a photo.

'An officer, eh, I bet you're proud too,' said the Ex Sergeant Major. Then the shit hit the fan.

'He was an officer in the Waffen SS.'

There it was, I couldn't believe it. Wocko held up a picture of his granddad, standing there, as proud as punch, giving it the full Nazi salute to the Fatherland. Shit, this isn't going to end well, I thought.

As Wocko's picture was passed from veteran to veteran, slowly the room went quiet. You could have heard a pin drop. For some reason the atmosphere changed drastically, there were no more smiles and the drinks stopped flowing. I thought that it would be a good time to head back to camp.

We quickly left the building and headed back to Bulwell Camp at a rapid pace, before they had time to put a posse together.

'What the fuck did you do that for? You're lucky you didn't get lynched,' I said as we walked quickly away from the legion.

'Yeah, I did get the feeling, showing them my picture didn't go down that well. It's a good job I didn't wear his medals,' Wocko answered.

'How the fuck did you end up with a German granddad?' I asked, glancing at Wocko as we walked along.

'My dad was in the British army. He met my mum when he was based in Germany. The picture was of her dad, when he was younger,' he replied.

Back in the room, the rest of the lads couldn't stop laughing, when I told them what had happened. I suppose it was funny looking back, but it wasn't funny at the time, not with a room full of military vets looking like they were about to rip Wocko's head off.

Chapter 3

Colchester Garrison

Colchester is said to be the oldest recorded town in Britain, and Colchester Garrison has been a military base since Roman times. The first recorded military unit to be based there was Legio XX Valeria Victrix (that's a mouthful) in 43AD, following the Roman invasion of Britain. Colchester also played an important role as a garrison town during the Napoleonic Wars and throughout the Victorian era.

The infantry in Colchester were housed in wooden huts, which served as barracks, between Mersea Road and Military Road until 1896. The huts were replaced by brick built barracks in 1896-1904, Hyderabad and Meeanee Barracks.

During WW1 several battalions of Kitchener's Army, were trained there. A lot of the old barracks and Victorian buildings have been demolished to make way for new barracks and housing. Now the 2nd Battalion and 3rd Battalion of The Parachute Regiment are based there.

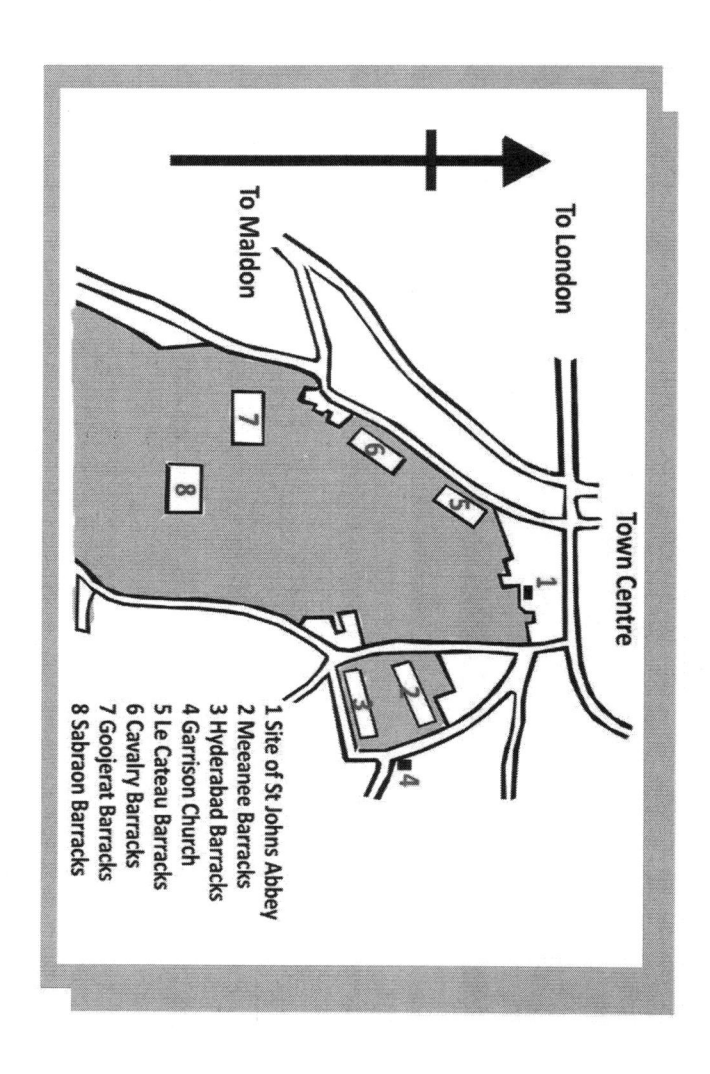

1 Site of St Johns Abbey
2 Meeanee Barracks
3 Hyderabad Barracks
4 Garrison Church
5 Le Cateau Barracks
6 Cavalry Barracks
7 Goojerat Barracks
8 Sabraon Barracks

SPARROW'S FART

A few days later, our short holiday on KAPE tour was over. We were all back at Meeanee barracks, Colchester. KAPE tour had been a welcome break from the routine, but now it was back to the weekly drill parades, early morning runs, guard duties, exercises and all that bullshit.

Our role in Colchester was air portable battalion, which meant we had to be ready to move anywhere in the world, at 24 hours' notice. In a week's time, we were to be tested in that role. We were being sent to Germany for a six-week exercise. Most of us had never been to Germany before, so we were all looking forward to it. But before that, we were all keen to get away on weekend leave to see our loved ones, if we were lucky.

It was now Monday morning 0545 hours, stupid o'clock. I'll always remember that dreaded noise of the strip lights being turned on by the duty NCO in his noisy ammo boots. That sudden bright light and the tinkling noise of the lights powering up one by one, and the words 'Wakey Wakey' or something a little stronger and less polite. We'd quickly jump into our Boots DMS, Denims, green placcy belt and red PT vest. Not forgetting the odd faded pink looking one, worn by the old sweat of the platoon.

> **Twisters**
>
> **To ensure that your Denims legs were tucked up, you could use elastic bands, knicker elastic, rubber waterproof seals from mortar bomb containers or Hoover belts, or, if the NAAFI stocked them, "hook on boot bands." Similar, to the twisters, that came later.**

Then it was on parade outside the block for our early morning beasting, running around Colchester Garrison. Out of the gates, turn left towards the old married quarters, then right heading towards the Garrison church, then on towards Cavalry Barracks.

> **I have a cunning plan Baldrick!!**

> Cavalry Barracks on the Circular Road North was built in 1863. The parade ground of the barracks was used for the opening credits of Blackadder Goes Forth and in a famous scene in Monty Python's, The Meaning of Life.

Some of us enjoyed the runs. For those who smoked forty fags a day, it was far from fun. It felt like your heart and lungs wanted to explode out of your chest. Then there were the fatties, who flaked out half way round. We even had one lad who couldn't make the guardroom on the way out. I think every platoon had one of those!

If we'd been on the piss the night before and had a few too many Pernod's, somewhere along the garrison tour we were reunited with last night's mushy peas and chips. Throwing up in a squaded run without breaking step was a skill. The poor sod in front who got it down his back wasn't happy though! Nor was the pebble dashed guy behind.

PTI's, "Ten times round my beautiful body...Go!"

All the time whilst we were on the run, we had to put up with cheesy comments from the 'Oooh I'm fucking gorgeous me' PTI's like…

'Come on ladies'… 'Pain is a sensation that lets us know we ain't dead yet.' And the poor stragglers at the back would really get it…'My grandmother can run faster than you lot, and she's only got one fucking leg.'

Areas

After the run was finished, all we wanted to do was get out of the cold, up to our room, and flake out on our pits. But no, it was then area cleaning, wombling around the block, picking up those nub ends, we'd been throwing out of the windows all weekend.

I'll never forget the smell of fags and sweat as we walked around the blocks, steam coming from our PT shirts, with our hands down our bollocks, trying to keep them warm, or sharing a cigarette with umpteen other blokes. Usually JPS or No6, cigarettes, with a long red end looking like a nuclear warhead.

'Don't walk fucking past it, pick the fucker up.' How many times do you remember hearing that, or was that you shouting it?

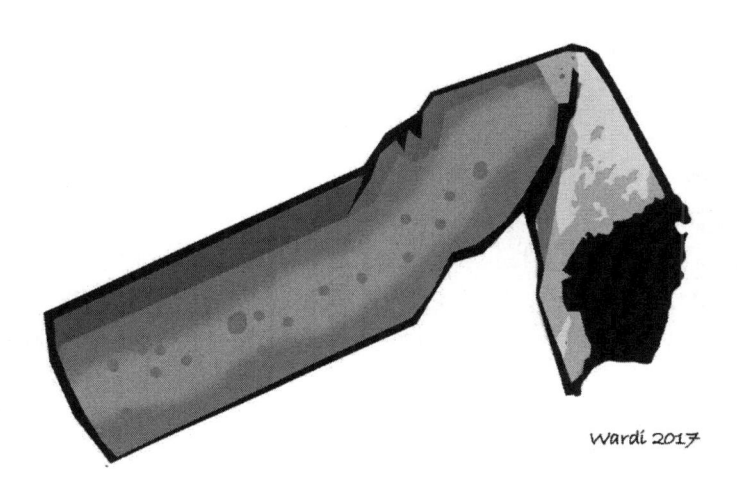

What do you mean you can't breathe... I cant play the piano, but I don't moan about it!! 2 days light duties, off you go!!

Of course, all this could be avoided, we could go sick! But the army was always one step ahead. If going sick was easy, half the battalion would be queuing up, down the med centre every time there was a run.

If we wanted to go sick, it was on parade down the guard room at 0700 hours or earlier, in full, No 2 dress, carrying our kidney pouches, complete with KFS, towels green for the use of, washing and shaving kit, survival kit, socks, pants and God knows what else. What was the point of that?

It didn't matter if we were dying. If we didn't pass sick parade inspection, we were sent back to our block to die. Then later the person's roommates, would find their dead body and say 'Look at him the wanker, he would do anything to avoid PT and the bastard owed me £50.'

Sadly, in most units, bullshit beats brains hands down. Can you imagine if civvies, had to go through that rigmarole when visiting the doctors, the NHS would save a fortune.

After recovering from the run, and before heading back to the room to complete the room jobs and get ready for the day's events, we had breakfast, 'Queens Parade': full-English breakfast and a large black mug full of tea.

Breakfast would keep us going until mid-morning, when it was NAAFI break, where we usually demolished a steak and kidney pie, a pint of milk and a cream bun, no messing. Hold on a second, hadn't we just had a full breakfast less than 2 hours, ago? An hour later, after NAAFI break, it was dinner time. So, it was back to the cook-house for a hearty dinner, which kept us going until tea time at 1630 hours. 'How did we do it?' At tea, whatever we had, was always accompanied by half a loaf of bread with 2 mugs of tea, one to drink there and one take back to the block, along with the 2 currant buns hidden in your Denims map pocket. Yes, that's what they were for. Let's face it, did anyone ever put a map in it?

And the eating didn't stop there. We always sent the new boy out on a fish and chip run or we all piled down the NAAFI, if we had money. The alcohol consumed must have added about an extra 2000 calories a day. Where the hell did we put it all? Being young has a lot going for it. No wonder we were beasted by the PTI's, most mornings.

After tea, we headed for the company office, to check part one orders and company detail, to find out what horrors we had to put up with the next day or week, before the trip to the Fatherland.

'Shit,' Doris said, 'I've only bagged a bloody church parade on Sunday, I wanted to go home this weekend. Fuck it! I'm not doing it', I'm an atheist for Christ sake!'

'You have to go Doris, Jesus will be really offended you know,' Wocko said, laughing.

> ## Garrison Church
>
> **Built back in 1854 it is the oldest surviving garrison building in Colchester, if not the UK or world.**
>
> **It was originally built as a hospital during the Crimean war.**

'I don't know what you're laughing at Wocko. You're on guard duty on Saturday,' Clarkey said, pointing to the guard list on company detail.

'What... Where? Bollocks, no way. I bet that's Sergeant Billings' doing, he fucking hates me.'

'It looks like it's just me, Clarkey, Doubles and Wardi going home this weekend, that's if we can survive RSM's drill parade,' Eddie said smiling.

'Don't worry, I'll be in that car, you can bet your life on it,' Wocko said, as we all entered our room.

Weekend Leave

Eddie was the only one with a car. Most weekends, if we got the chance, we'd all chip in for the petrol and head home. The alternative was to go by train. Going home by train from Colchester to the Midlands in some battered old British Rail carriage was a nightmare at the best of times, unless we paid to go via London, which was quicker, but cost an arm and a leg. If we used one of our train warrants, the army would send us by snail rail, sending us on the longest and cheapest route. Which meant half a dozen changes, and stopping at every station on the route, Colchester to Derby via fucking Scotland! Coming back wasn't much better either. We'd always catch the last train for some reason. It was a military thing, whatever branch we were in. It was one of three things; staying in the pub on a Sunday night as long, as we could, being with our girlfriends until the last possible minute, snogging their face off on the platform, or trying to grab every minute we could away from the barracks. When the last train did eventually set off, it was endless stops and with a bit of luck we'd get to the final station in time to make the last connection. I'd often find the odd military person sleeping in the luggage racks. They unscrewed the light bulbs so they could get some shut eye. Then panicking, they put them back in again when they heard the guard coming to check tickets. What amazed me was that I always made it back for breakfast 99% of the time.

If people were late for work in Civvy Street, usually they got away with it, or some mug would clock them in. Late for work in the army meant you were absent without leave, and could receive anything from 7 days, rippers, or the loss of up to 7 days, pay or both. It all depended on what mood the OC was in.

Back in our room, we were all lying on our bed's when Eddie decided to offer Wocko some advice.

'Why don't you have a word with Doubles, Wocko. He'll do your duty for you, for a price.'

Doubles Back

Every platoon had their characters, and our platoon was full of them. Accommodated in an 8 man, room, on the second floor, we had one TV, owned by a short stumpy guy nicknamed Doubles. Doubles had a reputation for being a tight arse. He was that tight that if you shoved a lump of coal up his arse, within hours you'd have a diamond. Doubles would always place his TV on his bedside locker, at such an angle that no one else could watch it, unless we paid him 20 pence a day. That changed one night when match of the day was on. We were all skint and couldn't pay him his 20 pence, so he wouldn't let us watch the football. When he went for a shit, Eddie got up, walked over to the TV and lobbed it out of the window. Being two floors up, the TV didn't stand a chance. Try as he might, he couldn't get a reception after that! He didn't say a word, and didn't talk to us for days.

The reason he ended up with the name Doubles, is because of his reputation for lending you anything for doubles back. Want money, doubles back. Want a train warrant, doubles back. Yes, I'll buy you a pint or a pie down the NAAFI, doubles back. I remember once on exercise he sold a single cigarette to Wocko for £5, that he had to pay him back on pay day. Five pounds was a lot of money back then, half a day's pay at least. I'm sure everyone had a Doubles in their unit. I bet they're all millionaires now. Doubles would always be willing to do a guard duty for the right price.

'Come on Doubles,' Wocko pleaded, 'do my guard duty for me.'

'Ten pounds,' Doubles said, holding out his hand.

'Ten bloody pounds, that's robbery. That will leave me nearly skint.'

'You'll make me cry in a minute, Wocko,' Doubles answered.

'I've heard you're that tight, you only cry out of one eye anyway Doubles,' Eddie said.
'I'll give you five pounds,' Wocko replied.
'Eight pounds, that's the lowest I'll go, take it or leave it.'
'Ok, ok, eight pounds then. You're a fucking rob dog Doubles.'
About a minute went by, and Wocko was still standing in Doubles' bed space.
'What is it now Wocko, why are you still standing there. I said I'd do it, didn't I?'
'You couldn't lend us £8, could you?'
'Doubles back,' Doubles said, reaching into his locker.
'Ok, doubles back,' Wocko agreed.
'That's £16 on pay day then Wocko,' Doubles replied, as he made a note of the agreement in the writing pad he'd taken from his locker.
'That's why you've never got any money, you're an idiot Wocko,' I said, shaking my head in disbelief.
'It's my money. I can do what I want with it,' Wocko answered, sounding aggrieved.

Suited and Booted

'Right, you lot listen up,' Sergeant Billings said, as he entered the room. 'The OC is pissed off with his men going home on leave in scruff order, looking like a bag of shit. As from today if you want to go home at the weekend, you cannot leave barracks unless you are wearing a suit and tie. So, for all you lucky enough to fuck off home to mummy, the PC and I want you all stood by your beds, suited and booted, ready for inspection on Friday. I will not tolerate individuals who are dirty, untidy and living like pigs. I expect high standards at all, times. If you're not up to scratch, you won't be going anywhere, is that clear? Have you got that Watkinson, you do have a suit, don't you?'

'Yes, Sergeant.'

Sergeant Billings peered into Wocko's, locker. The smell hit him like a brick wall. It affected him that badly he started to cough.

'You'll be surprised what you'll find in there, Sergeant, it's like an Aladdin's cave,' Eddie said smirking.

'Watkinson, you are one disgusting specimen. Are you trying to start a Bio-nuclear war by any chance? Make sure it's not smelling and looking like that on Friday, or you won't be going anywhere, suit or no suit.'

'Do I have to wear a suit Sergeant, I'm not going home, I'm on church parade on Sunday,' Doris said.

'No, you can wear No2 dress, Day. That goes for all of you, if you haven't got a suit, it's, No2 dress. See you tomorrow gents,' Sergeant Billings said, as he exited the room.

'What did you ask him that for Doris, now we all have to wear No2 dress,' Clarkey moaned.

'Have you really got a suit Wocko? I find that hard to believe,' Eddie said.

'Yes, I have got a suit, it was my dad's, it's in here

somewhere,' Wocko said, looking, in his locker, scratching his head.

With Doubles doing Wocko's duty, we were back to four in the car on Friday, but we knew there would be more casualties, there always were.

Chapter 4

In front of all the accommodation blocks, we had huge grassy areas about the size of half a football pitch. Walking over those grassy areas would mean a shorter route to the cook-house to beat the queue, but be warned, if anyone chose to run the gauntlet, they ventured into those areas at their peril. As we all know, all RSM's would have kittens if they caught anyone strolling across their sacred ground, the parade square, but if they caught them walking on the grass, they'd go fucking ballistic. Walking around camp in working hours, we were always on the lookout, it always seemed like the RSM was around the next corner, just waiting to pounce on us. Even if he was sitting in his bath at home, he'd still catch us, the sneaky fucker. The sound of his ammo boots scraping on the ground, coming from around the corner, forced us to change direction sharpish.

On that Tuesday, at dinner time, it was our very own Corporal Clarke, who decided to run the gauntlet, and guess what, he was caught bang to rights, in the centre of the grass square by the Regimental Sergeant Major.

Suddenly the mouth of hell opened, up. All we could hear for miles around belting out at about 110 decibels was, 'Get the fuck off my grass, only two people walk on the grass in this camp, me and God, and God is on R&R. Get off my grass, you worthless piece of shit. YES, YOU!'

Poor Clarkey had nowhere to go. Red faced looking like he'd been caught parking in a handicapped space, he was marooned. He had 20 yards of grass all around him. What could he do? Call a helicopter and get airlifted out of there? What happened next had us all rolling around with laughter.

Trying his hardest not to upset the RSM anymore, Clarkey thought he had only one option: he started to take huge steps to limit his contact with the RSM's precious grass. To see Clarkey leaping across the grass like some sort of demented frog, while at the same time taking the RSM's barrage of abuse, was hilarious.

'You are still on my grass, move like you've got a purpose in life Corporal, you fucking cretin! Get off my grass, take one more step on my grass. Are you stupid... you are stupid... you're so fucking stupid!

You go way beyond stupid. We're now into a whole new fucking different dimension of stupid....'

Clarkey was the first casualty. His punishment was to join Doris on church parade, no weekend leave for him, now it was just the three of us.

The next couple of days flew by, it was now Thursday, the best day of the week, payday, plus we knew the weekend was approaching fast. That evening, after a few beers down the NAAFI, we went back to the room to prepare our kit, buffing our brasses, bulling our boots for the RSM's drill parade. After we'd done that, we had a room inspection to prepare for, which meant room jobs, tidying up our lockers and the dreaded polishing and buffing of the floors. The night before a room inspection was always written off.

Wocko was busy plastering the inside of his locker with porn.

'What do you reckon lads? My locker looks well smart, doesn't it?'

'Wocko you are supposed to be tidying your locker up, getting rid of the filth, not covering your locker with it,' I said.

'I don't know, I think it's an improvement, especially that blonde above your mirror,' Eddie said.

Join the army see the world and clean it.

I hated the smell of that orangey, yellow, gunk floor polish, we were given to use. The smell of that polish would linger for days. It was going to be a long night. Because I was still relatively new to the platoon, I ended up doing most of the work, while Eddie, the old sweat, spent most of the time on his pit, reading his grot mag, and dishing out the orders.

'You missed a bit Wardi, I can't hear that bumper swinging,' he said, still ogling the pictures in his magazine.

'Mucking in, isn't a pub in China, you know Eddie,' I replied feeling pissed off.

'You'll go far, you will Wardi. As long, as transport is laid on,' he laughed.

The hand bumper, who can forget the sound of the double clicking, as you swung it from side to side, with your torn piece of grey blanket underneath for extra shine? If you didn't have a bumper you just improvised, by being dragged around in an old blanket, trying to get the floor to shine. What about

the hours spent using Brasso on radiator valves, taps, and door panels, why?
During room cleaning, Doris would always go missing and Wocko was a waste of fucking time. With King Midas, everything he touched turned to gold, in Wocko's case everything he touched turned to shite. At least Doubles did his fair share, and we didn't have to pay him this time!

> The next one who moves, I will stick my boot so far up your ass that your breath will smell like Kiwi.

RSM's drill parade

It was now Friday, 1310 hours, twenty minutes before RSM's drill parade. The whole company had fell in outside the company office, ready for the order to march onto the parade square. Usually accompanied by the Band and Drums playing marching tunes, like 'Great little army' and 'Colonel Bogey'.
The dress code for the RSM's drill parade was: a

beret, bulled toe capped DMS boots, KF shirt, jumper, heavy wool and starched barrack room trousers. The plastic barrack dress trousers would either fuck your steam iron up, or the iron would melt them. We secured it altogether with our green placcy belts over the top of our jumper. We looked well smart. Looking back now we looked totally stupid. Did they think the belts served a practical purpose? Belts should be used to hold up Keck's, but back then, it sort of felt right.

The parade usually lasted about an hour. The key to survival was that you make sure you didn't get singled out. If you were slightly out with your timing on a drill movement, your life was over. The RSM would be breathing down your neck in milliseconds. Your drill had to be better than the moves on Strictly Come Dancing. If it was this bad for us, what was it like for the Guards Regiments? Did everybody have a 'Tash' back then? You could be the smartest soldier on parade, but the RSM would still find a reason to send you down the road to the guard room. It didn't matter what rank you were either, he'd still give you a dressing down.

Elvis

He had a habit of walking up and down the ranks saying, 'jail him, haircut, charged, jail him, haircut, charged.' He was always followed by a posse of regimental police, carrying out his orders like a bunch of trainee chefs, following Gordon Ramsey in Hell's kitchen. That afternoon, I thought my number was up. He walked past me then stopped and walked backwards about three paces, and ripped into the guy next to me. He looked down his nose at this guy, as though he had just stepped in shit.

'How can you be so ugly with only one head? While we are on the subject, of heads, what the fuck is that on yours?'

He was referring to the guy's un-shrunken beret.

'You are supposed to stand underneath your beret, not beside it, sort it out.'

Suddenly his face was about three millimetres away from mine. 'You've got to be fucking kidding me?' He started to go mental about the length of my sideburns. 'Who the fuck, do you think you are? Fucking Elvis? I bet you'd like to keep those sideburns, wouldn't you?'

I didn't say a word. I knew whatever I said would be wrong.

'I'll get you a fucking bag to put them in, shall I? Those sideburns are far too fucking long.' Then he took a closer look and smiled.

'Wait a minute; they're not fucking sideburns. They're just long strands of hair pretending to be fucking sideburns. How old are you soldier, fucking 12?' Using his, finger he pushed them behind my ears. Then he started to laugh.

'That's better,' he said, as he walked away.

I'd dodged a bullet. I was lucky, I'd made it, there was always a handful that didn't. Even the married pads weren't safe. Some of them would find themselves in jail for the whole weekend.

I remember one of the married guy's wives turning up at the guardroom, demanding that they release her husband. She was approached by the RSM, who told her if she didn't go away, he would jail her too, along with her three kids and the pet dog.

The RSM's drill parade was over. We'd all made it. Just the PC's inspection to go now and we'd be on our way home.

Urban Myth alert

There was even a rumour that the RSM threatened to jail his own 12, year old, daughter for wearing mixed dress, after she was sent home from school for wearing pink trainers, instead of black shoes with her school uniform.

As we all know, RSM's hated long hair and this RSM was no different. He used to say, 'gentlemen whatever is inside your beret is yours, whatever is outside your beret is mine.'

This was the late 70's. There was one occasion when he singled out one of our many black guys, pointed his pace stick at the soldier's beret and flicked it off. That was it, all hell broke loose, when his massive afro style hairdo sprang out like a jack-in-a-box. The RSM was for the first time, lost for words.

The Gun Fight at the Ok Corral

As I wandered past the company office heading for my block, I heard a familiar voice.

'Ward, get in my office. I want a word with you,' said Johnny Jap, our Company Sergeant Major.

He was a short guy, friendly most of the time, with a good sense of humour, but if you crossed him you knew about it. This bloke was destined to be the next RSM. If he wanted to, he could reduce you down to a midget. There must be a course they all go on to learn how to do that! What have I done now, I thought? I stood nervously in front of his desk while he sat down, then he reached under his desk.

'Is this yours Ward?' the CSM asked, holding up a 22, air rifle.

Earlier in the week I'd bought a 22, air rifle from Eddie for £10, bargain I thought. I thought wrong, now I was about to find out why. Deny everything, I thought.

'No, sir.'

'Don't fucking lie to me Ward. Do you realise having a firearm in your, locker is a chargeable offence? All weapons are supposed to be kept in the armoury.'

I knew then someone had tipped them off about my new purchase.

'It's only a 22, air rifle sir. It's hardly going to kill anyone,' I replied.

'Really... Are you prepared to pay for the £600's worth of damage your pop gun has caused to the C Company accommodation block then?' the CSM asked.

I was confused. What the hell was he talking about? I hadn't even fired it yet.

'I'm sure you'll be interested to know that the block resembles a scene from the film The Gun Fight at the Ok Corral.'

I didn't know it at the time, but unluckily for me, I was last in a chain of previous owners of this air rifle. For the last few weeks while we were on KAPE tour, the bastards had been playing war games around the accommodation block. There were pellet holes everywhere, mainly in locker doors, where squaddies had been defending themselves from a mass *shoot me up.* I'm sure there must have been more pop guns involved.

Bumpers & Bed Blocks

'Well, Billy the *fucking* Kid... I know you weren't the first person to own this air rifle. What I want to know is who gave it to you, or sold it to you?' the CSM said.

What could I say, it was a catch 22, situation. I either told him it was Eddie, or I took the rap. I pondered for a while and said,

'I don't know anything about any air rifle. Somebody must have planted it in my locker, while I was at the cook-house having my scran.'

'So, you left your locker open?'

'Err, I must have done, sir,' I said, knowing that leaving your locker open unattended, meant a bollocking at the very least.

'I don't have to remind you Private Ward it is your responsibility to make sure you secure all your personal and military property under lock and key. Failure to do so is a chargeable offence.' He sat back in his chair, folded his arms and gave me a sarcastic smile.

He knew I was lying, and he knew who sold me the weapon. There was no way I'd grass anyone up, especially not my best mate Eddie. My life wouldn't be worth living.

'Get out my fucking office. If I find out you've lied to me Ward, I'll be on you like a tramp on chips. Oh, and by the way, you're on officer's mess duties this weekend, as punishment for leaving you locker open, and tell Edwards he can join you.'

I did a quick about turn and left his office as fast as I could. I arrived back at the room and confronted Eddie.

'What did the CSM want you for Wardi?' Eddie asked, smiling.

'You know exactly what he wanted. That bloody air rifle you sold me, it's been around the whole fucking company. There's more pellet holes than fucking wood-worm holes in this block.'

'Sorry Wardi, I didn't know, honest. You didn't tell him anything, did you?'

'No, of course I didn't, but guess what? We're both on officers, mess duties this weekend.'

'You're kidding me,' Eddie said, looking downcast.

Wocko started to laugh, 'so, I'm the only one going home this weekend.'

Oliver Twist

Later that day, we were all stood by our beds, waiting for the Platoon Commander to arrive for his inspection, and the only one wearing a suit was Wocko! Corporal Clarke brought the room to attention as the PC and Sergeant Billings entered the room. The PC expected most of us to be dressed in suits, ready for weekend leave.

'What's this?' asked the PC, 'I take it none of you want to go home this weekend.'

'Most of the men are on duty, sir, apart from Watkinson,' Corporal Clark replied.

The PC made a bee-line for Wocko. Looking him up and down, he couldn't believe what he was seeing. Wocko was stood to attention, smiling, looking like a chimney sweep, in his ill, fitting, black top hat and tails.

'Take that smile off your face Watkinson. What on earth are you wearing man, you look widiculous. Is this a wind up, Sergeant Billings?' the PC asked.

'Explain Watkinson' Sergeant Billings said.

'The suit was my dad's sir, he's was an undertaker.'

The PC stood there open mouthed. While everybody in the room was trying their hardest not to burst out laughing.

'Watkinson words fail me, you look like one of the cast from Oliver Twist. Is this a joke?'

'My dad died, sir, the suit was left to me in his will. It's the only thing I have that belonged to him. It means a lot to me.'

Sergeant Billings sniffs the air. 'So, that's what that smell is, is it? Was he still wearing it when he died, or is that smell coming from your locker? Wherever it's coming from it stinks that bad, it's sucking me fucking in. It's alive, save me Watkinson... Hold on, your old man... he's not in there, is he?' Sergeant Billings said.

The PC didn't look happy and he took Sergeant Billings to one side. 'I think that's a bit below the belt don't you Sergeant Billings? After all, that's his father you're talking about.'

'Permission to speak, sir. Sergeant Billings is right, he is in there,' Wocko said, with a proud look on his face.

The PC and Sergeant Billings looked confused. Wocko then did an about turn, bent down, and pulled out his dad's ashes from the bottom of his locker. He then presented the urn to the PC.

'There you go, sir, I rescued it from my mum. She was only going to take it to the local jumble sale.'

'Watkinson, I don't know what to say. Get that thing out of my sight, you're unbelievable,' the PC said.

Sergeant Billings then whispered in Watkinson ear. 'You think I was born yesterday, don't you Watkinson? I know your game. You thought covering your locker with porn would distract me from noticing what a fucking mess your locker is in. You're nothing but a living argument for euthanasia at birth. I hope one day you will go back to the fucking swamp you came from, and fucking stay there, you walking cesspit. What's red and white and goes up and down Watkinson?'

'I don't know Sergeant.'

'The barrier at the main gate, you're on guard duty this weekend.'

> **Who can remember this?**
> 'If you stag on this weekend, I'll give you Monday off.'

The PC then addressed the room. 'Listen in gentlemen, whatever you do this weekend, enjoy yourself and wemember, Monday we are off to Germany for a 6, week exercise. When we get there, I expect 100% commitment for the whole time we are there. I think we need to hit the gwound wunning, keep our eye on the ball, and make sure that we are singing from the same song-sheet. Cawwy on Sergeant Billings.'

Sergeant Billings' brief was straight to the point, 'right listen up. By all means, enjoy yourselves tonight, but don't tear the fucking arse out of it. Come Monday morning, I want you on parade outside the block at 1030 hours ready for inspection, with all your gear. Your kit list is on the notice board, make sure you read it. We leave for Germany at 1200 hours, any questions? No, good!'

Sergeant Billings and the PC left the room.

'Well, that's it, none of us will be going home this weekend,' Clarkey sighed.

'It's not fair. I've already sold one guard duty, now I've got another one. I'm confused.'

'Sorry Wocko, I can't do that one as well,' Doubles said.

'Ask your dad, if he'll do it for you Wocko,' Doris

joked.

'I can't believe I've been sleeping next to your dead dad's ashes all this time. How long has your old man been in there, Wocko?' Eddie asked.

'Oh about 6 months, but why should it bother you, it's only a pot of ashes.'

'It hasn't bothered me. I'm only pissed off because I've gone without an ashtray all this time, when I could have borrowed yours,' Eddie laughed.

'Very, funny Eddie,' Wocko said, as he put his dad's ashes back in his locker. 'There you go pop, take no notice of them.'

'So, what are we going to do gents, we've still got tonight off?' Eddie said.

Nobody spoke. Most of us were pissed off because we wanted to go home.

'Come on lads, it's not that bad, it's Friday night. Are we just going to sit around the block all night, then, drinking beer and watching porn, there must be more to life, than that!' Eddie tried to cheer us up.

For a few seconds, there was total silence. Then Wocko opened his mouth.

'Well, I can't think of anything,' Wocko said.

Out on the town

Barrack life is what we made it. Nowadays they have everything, wireless internet access, gymnasiums, car clubs, sports facilities etc. Back then on weekdays, it was doss in our room or down the NAAFI for a pint or the occasional grab a granny night in town. That was it. At weekends, if we were stuck in camp and had a few quid left over from pay day, most squaddies would head downtown with the lads, on the lash, taking every opportunity to shag anything with a pulse. Staying in the barracks on a Friday night was unheard of, unless the person was skint, on duty or an orphan. Once we were outside those camp gates, we had no problem with pulling girls. It didn't matter if we looked like the elephant man, women of all ages and sizes, young and old, would appear from everywhere, as long, as we had a fat wallet. Those garrison girls knew when we were getting paid before we did, skint civvies were just pushed to one side. That's why most of them wanted to start fights.

In Colchester, the places to go back then were THE ROYAL STANDARD just outside the camp gates on Mersea road (shut down now). Heading into town you passed another pub, forget what it was called, mainly the senior ranks went in there. At the bottom of Mersea road, near the roundabout was THE FOUNTAIN, next door to the rip-off tattooist shop. But the place to be and where most squaddies ended up on a Friday and Saturday night, was THE WAGON AND HORSES, where often huge fights would break out between blokes from two or three different units laying claim to it as "their" pub. Another place where we could hang out, was THE GRAPES NIGHT CLUB. Of course, there were lots more places to go, but these are the ones I can remember from the mid-seventies.

Clive Ward

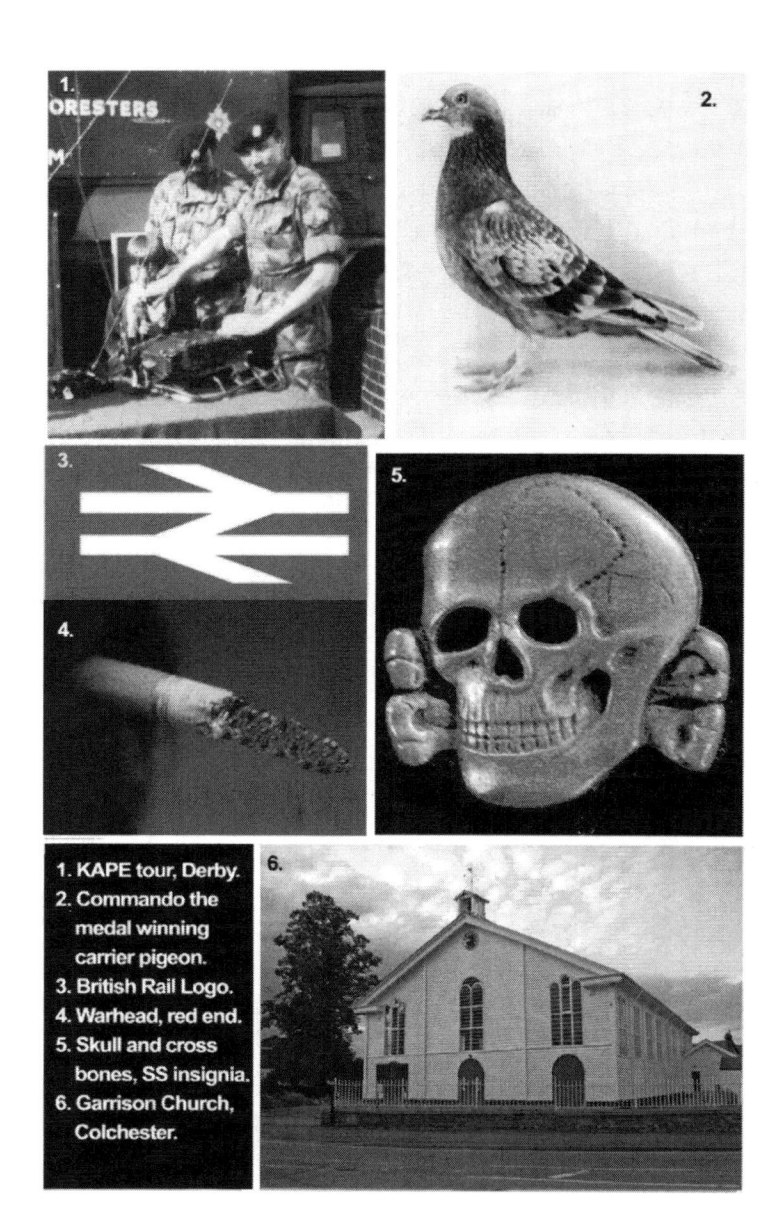

1. KAPE tour, Derby.
2. Commando the medal winning carrier pigeon.
3. British Rail Logo.
4. Warhead, red end.
5. Skull and cross bones, SS insignia.
6. Garrison Church, Colchester.

Bumpers & Bed Blocks

1. The entrance to the M.C.T.C.
2. Wocko's Dad's ashes.
3. Twisters.
4. Officers Mess Meeanee Barracks, Colchester.
5. Compo rations from the 1970's, matches, boiled sweets and oatmeal blocks etc.

Birds and Bees

As usual that Friday, we all started to get ready for a night on the town, apart from Doris and Wocko. They had both decided to stay in camp.

'Come on Doris get ready,' Eddie urged.

'You're ok lads. I think I'll give it a miss, thanks. Anyway, I've got bible studies to do for Sunday.'

'Don't be a twat Doris. We all know why you don't want to go on the pull. When was the last time you had a jump?' Eddie asked.

'Um... isn't it time for tea yet?' Doris replied, as colour suffused his cheeks.

'Come on, out with it.' Eddie was determined to get an answer.

'Leave him alone, Eddie,' Clarkey said.

'Spill the beans.' Eddie, wouldn't let it rest.

'Erm,' Doris muttered, looking like he wanted the ground to open and swallow him up.

'I know why, you're a virgin aren't you Doris?' Eddie said, pointing at him.

'No, I'm not! I've pulled lots of times,' Doris replied, going even redder in the face.

'Sorry Doris, wanking doesn't count,' Eddie joked.

'Take no notice of him Doris, you are who you are. You're saving yourself for the right one, aren't you?' I said, hoping to put an end to his torment.

'That's right, yes I am.' Doris looked relieved that someone had spoken up for him.

Eddie sat down on Doris's bed, who was pretending

to read a book trying to ignore him.

'It's alright Doris, I was just messing about. Why don't you let your uncle Eddie tell you about the birds and the bees!'

Then Wocko chose to butt in. 'Don't be silly Eddie. How can a tiny bee shag a big feathery bird? Besides the birds would get stung, wouldn't they?'

'Do you know something Wocko? You're so thick, you could get locked in the NAAFI and still starve to death. Shut the fuck up!' Eddie wasn't happy about being interrupted.

'Ok, I'll come, just leave me alone now please!' Doris said.

'Good lad, that's the spirit,' Eddie replied, patting him on the back.

'Eh Eddie, why don't we introduce Doris to Slacky Jackie,' Clarkey added, with a smile.

'Good thinking Clarkey.'

'Err, no thanks, you can keep your Slacky Jackie,' Doris said.

'What about you Wocko, are you coming?' Eddie asked.

'Not this time. Doubles has had all my money and I've got nothing to wear.'

'I'll buy you a few pints Wocko. Why don't you wear your dad's suit? You'd, definitely pull, wearing that, the girls will be all over you. Take your dad, he will make a good ice breaker.'

'Don't encourage him Wardi, it's not Halloween, and anyway, he'd never get past the guard room wearing that.'

Jumping off his bed, Wocko headed for the washroom. 'I'm not saying no to free beer, I'm coming.'
'I don't believe it, he's having a bath. What is the world coming to? Steady on Wocko,' Eddie said.
'Anyone want my water?' Wocko asked.
'Are you kidding, even Green peace wouldn't enter those waters,' Eddie replied.

> **Fact**
>
> **You always waited until all your roommates had gone down town before having a bath, otherwise a bucket of ice cold water would join you soon after getting in.**

After scraping together some clothes for Wocko, we all headed downtown. The aim that night was to get Doris set up on a blind date with Slacky Jackie, for a price! Knowing that some of us had to report for guard duty at 0530 hours the next morning we didn't stay out for long. We were already in bed half asleep before Doris and Clarkey appeared. Arriving back around midnight, Doris was grinning like a Cheshire cat.
'Doris, you dirty stop out... well?' Eddie said, turning his bedside light on.
'Well, what?'
'Tell me all about it, then'
'About what, oh you mean the girl I cracked off with

and you didn't.'
'Did you shag it?'
'Actually, we went to the pictures.'
'Then what happened?'
'Bambi's Mum got shot.'
'No, you idiot, what happened when you left the pictures?'
'We went for a walk in the park.'
'And... and'
'We sat on a bench.'
'And.'
'We kissed.'
'So, did you get laid?'
'No, I walked her to the taxi rank and she went home.'
'Ha... I knew it. I knew you weren't up to it, you haven't popped your cherry, have you? Everybody shags Slacky Jackie on the first date.'

Clarkey started to laugh as he spoke up in defence of Doris, 'Actually, Eddie, I spoke to Jackie before she got in the taxi, she said she really liked Graham. She also said she loves a man who can carry 2 pints of larger and 10 inches of onion rings at the same time, but there was no way she was going to let his 12, inch monster inside her tonight. She also said she'd rather have that than your 2 inches, any day of the week.'

Eddie didn't think it was funny. Without saying a word, he turned off his light and went to sleep, ignoring the laughing and sniggering.

Chapter 5

Guard Duties

It was now Saturday morning, 0500 hours. Wocko and Doubles were up and about, getting ready for guard duty. There was crap everywhere, clothes, beer cans, half eaten burgers. The place was a pig sty, a complete transformation from the previous day. It would stay like that all weekend, but by 0800 hours Monday, you could guarantee it would be back up to standard.

'Turn that fucking light off Wocko,' Clarkey shouted, before snuggling under his blankets.

'Yeah, hurry up with the light,' I said, burying my head under the pillow.

They didn't give a shit. They had to get up for a 24, hour duty, and they were going to make as much noise as possible.

The hours between 0600 and 0700 hours, were always a dangerous time on a Saturday or Sunday morning. If we were lucky, sometimes we'd get a tip off that the guard was one or two men short at Guard Mount. Then it was hide and seek before the press gang led by the guard 2 IC arrived, ordering us out of bed to make up the numbers and do a guard. We had no choice, we had to do it, and if we refused we'd end up down there anyway, but in jail as one of the inmates. One way of getting away with it, was to pretend to be still pissed from the night before. I tried that once and failed miserably, I wasn't a very good actor.

I remember guard duty like it was yesterday; that yellow floor polish smell again, the stick man, which I never got at guard mount, there was always someone with a smarter beret than me. Then there were the guard boxes, thrown together by the duty cook.

Every guard box had rock hard sugar and coffee, a lump of cheese, corn beef and tomato-*fucking*-sandwiches, that tasted rank because the tomato had made the bread go soggy, and the smelly 10 day old, boiled egg, which would come back to haunt you at about 3 in the morning. The lot was probably the rejects from horror bags, or they'd been sitting in the cook-house for the last few days.

> **Who can remember being pissed off because you'd pulled the 0200-0400 stag, then waking up at 0200 hours with a mouth like Gandhi's, flip flop.**

I don't know about anyone else, but as soon as we left the warm confines of the guard room, it was head for the block to find a warm drying room, or somewhere we wouldn't get caught, to have forty winks. I think we'd be unlucky to get caught, the only thing that could go wrong, and it did, was if we overstayed our welcome in the drying room, and overlaid. Then we were really in the shit. Nobody was late back from their stag, unless they'd been sleeping.

Picture the scene. It's now 0400 hours and we're trying to get that last hour in, before 0500 hours when the lights would go on and the bumper would start swinging. The prisoners were already up cleaning their cells and making up the dreaded bed blocks, that they thought they'd left behind in training. Then we'd hear, the sound of the regimental policeman blabbering out.
...'JEFDITEJEFDITEJEFDITEJEFDITEJEFDITEJEF DITEJEFDITE' as he marches his prisoners off to sweep the square, at a stupid pace that no one could keep up with. I know, I tried it a few times.......

Punishment

Who can forget the hours of fun reading the Incident Book? Some of the entries would go back to national service days. Reading some of those entries were the funniest and most shocking things, I've ever heard.
  I remember one incident, about a drunk soldier, who'd just arrived back in camp after a night on the piss. On the way to his block, he suddenly sprang a leak and got caught pissing on the regimental flag pole, unfortunately for him it was bad timing. The RSM just happened to be standing behind him, having just left the sergeants mess. He received 7 days in jail.
  Another lad got in trouble for misplacing his rifle, he also received 7 days in jail, but while he was inside, he was made to carry around a short section of telegraph pole by the RP's, everywhere he went. It must have weighed around 50lbs. He had to take it to the cook-house, to the bogs, even had to sleep with it. He didn't lose his weapon again!
  For the really, naughty boys, a few miles down the road we had the MCTC.

The Glass House

The Military Corrective Training Centre in Colchester, was previously used as a wartime Prisoner of War Camp. Although it is not classed as a prison, that's where squaddies were sent for the more serious offences. Today I think the maximum stay there is 24 months, depending on the seriousness of the crime. If it was a serious crime, they were housed there until they were transferred to Civilian prison. I don't know what the maximum stay was back in the 1970's and before, but I know it was a scary place to get sent. If someone were unlucky enough to be sent there, and their mum or girlfriend wondered why their address had suddenly changed to MCTC, and asked what it stood for, the inmate would tell them that it meant 'MARINE COMMANDO TRAINING CENTRE' or the 'MOTOR CYCLE TRAINING COLLEGE,' that was another good one. My betting is nearly all of us ex-military have swerved past a trip there. It is only those who get caught, who go.

Urban Myth

They say almost all RSM's had done at least one tour of the MCTC. That must be why they turn out to be bastards.

Chapter 6

Germany Bound

The rest of that weekend flew by, it was now Monday morning. We were all stood on parade outside our block. Sergeant Billings had just completed his kit inspection when the PC arrived.

'Everything ok Sergeant Billings, are we all weady and pwesent?'

'Yes, sir, apart from Watkinson.'

'Why, where is he?'

'I've just told him he can't take his dad to Germany with him. He's taken him back to the block.'

'The poor lad, I think we need to get the padwe to have a word with him. He's obviously not wight Sergeant.'

Sergeant Billings gave the PC an incredulous look and shook his head.

'Good morning men,' said the PC, 'I hope you all enjoyed your weekend.'

'Yes, sir, Doris pulled sir, didn't you Doris,' Eddie said, trying to keep a straight face.

The PC looked puzzled and turned to Sergeant Billings.

'Sergeant Billings enlighten me, will you. What does he mean by *pulled*?'

'Pulled sir, scored, copped off, sir.'
'I still don't know what you mean.'
'It means he's found himself a member of the opposite sex sir, and no doubt she's a right trollop.'
'*Twollop*? Oh, I see. Good for you Day, did anyone else *pull*?'
'Yes, sir, all of us all weekend, our right hands are killing us, sir,' Eddie replied, grinning.
'Alright, alright, that's enough.. Right grab your kit and horror bags and get on the bus,' Sergeant Billings said.

Departure

After what seemed like ages, we arrived at RAF Brize Norton. Then it was the customary hurry up and waiting, moving from hanger to hanger, waiting for our crab air flight. We finally boarded our VC10. After a short plane journey, we arrived in Germany. Then we were moved on to white buses for the journey to Rheinsehlen Camp.

We slept for most of the journey to Rheinsehlen Camp. All I can remember, was waking up to find I only had one sweaty cheese sandwich and half a bottle of flat panda pop left in my horror bag, but it wasn't wasted, Wocko soon put that away.

Soltau-Lüneburg Training Area

Following an agreement between the Federal German Republic, Canada and the UK that was made in 1959, the British and Canadian military, used the area to train their armies from 1963 until 1994.

With the Red Army on their doorstep during the cold war, the Federal German government, allowed Canada and the UK to use the area of Soltau-Lüneburg, to train their troops, so, they could defend Germany in the event of an attack. The British and Canadian's were also told they could not use their military vehicles on Sundays or public holidays.

Rheinsehlen Camp

One day you could be freezing your nuts off, on another day it was like the Somme 1916, wet and muddy, and in the summer, it was one big dust bowl.

There were dozens of Nissen huts in rows, on either side of the road and other buildings; because of the amount of troops taking part in the exercise, we had the luxury of being accommodated in tents, row after row of them. Thankfully, they were already erected by the advance party. This was my first visit to the camp, although there were many after that. Eddie, Wocko and Clarkey had done a stint at Soltau in the early seventies, so they knew what to expect, unlike the rest of us. But what I remember most about Rheinsehlen Camp, apart from its swampy shower blocks, were the Roman style toilet blocks, situated near the camp air strip. With the sound of constant running water, underneath them, a dozen thunder boxes faced another dozen thunder boxes, with no partitions. We could sit in those bogs all day chatting, and shitting, away our compo, to our heart's content. It's even been said, it's where the first ever Mexican wave started.

Urban Myth

It is said, after the Nazis came to power in 1933, and the Deutsche Luftwaffe where based there in 1938, that Hitler himself and his cronies visited those very bogs at Rheinsehlen Camp for a dump. I can just imagine Joseph Goebbels chatting away to his boss. 'Eh Adolf, you didn't tell me you only had one bollock!'

Bumpers & Bed Blocks

"You didn't tell me you only had one ball!"

While we were busy accommodating our stuff in the assigned tents, Doris went to check out the facilities. When he came back from his excursion his face had a gloomy expression.

'I can't believe it, I've just checked out those bogs. They're like something out of the dark ages. I'm dying for a crap, but there's no fucking way I'm sitting there while someone else is taking a crap right next to me or facing me. That's bloody disgusting that is, who would do that?' Doris complained.

'I sleep next to Wocko's locker every night, so I'm immune to all that,' I said.

'Don't be such a twat Doris. Everyone, has to take a crap, what's wrong with you? What're you going to do, go without having a dump for 6 weeks?' Eddie asked.

'I'll just have to go later, when it gets dark, nobody will want to go then,' Doris replied.

'What about wanking, that's going to be

embarrassing,' Wocko added.

For a second, nobody said a word, and just stared at Wocko, unable to believe what he'd just said.

'For fuck's sake Wocko, the tone of the conversation was low enough, did you have to lower it even further,' I said.

'I was just saying that's all. I'll just have to knock one out in my sleeping bag, won't I.'

'You wank in your maggot?' Clarkey sounded scandalised.

'Of course, I do, don't you? Everyone wanks in their sleeping bag... don't they?'

It was a tumbleweed blowing across the desert moment. We all stopped what we were doing and stared at Wocko waiting for his next word.

'Sometimes I even make a little hole.' Wocko added.

'OK, ok Wocko, too much information.' It was time to stop, apply my safety catch and step away from the conversation.

One fucking sausage

16.30 hours scran time, we all headed for the cookhouse. On arrival, the queue was massive. As usual out came the one liners.

'Bloody hell! You could starve to death standing here. Surely the grubs not that good.'

'I wonder if we could get VIP passes.'

After a long wait, we eventually got to the front of the queue.

'This better be worth the wait,' I said.

'Watch out! Here comes portion control,' Doubles joked.
'One fucking sausage,' said the fat slop jockey sergeant brandishing his ladle.

Never understood why they rationed us to one of this and one of that. If there wasn't enough for seconds, how come the slop bins were nearly always full?

We got served and sat down to eat our grub. It turned out it wasn't worth the wait.
 'This grub is disgusting, have we really got to live on this shite for the next six weeks? I'm going to starve,' Doubles complained.
 'I don't know what you're moaning about? This is a well, balanced meal,' Eddie replied, as he shovelled the food into his mouth.
 'Yeah with a fifty-fifty survival rate,' I added.

'Enjoy it while you can lads,' said Clarkey, 'once we get out there on exercise, we'll be living on good old compo.'

'Anything's better than this stuff,' Doubles moaned.

'Will you shut the fuck up Doubles? It's like you're on permanent send. We've had worse experiences in a cook-house, haven't we Wocko? Remember Montgomery Barracks 74?' Eddie said.

Montgomery Barracks

Montgomery Barracks was built between 1935-39 and served as a school for the signal wing of the Luftwaffe.
The barracks fell to the Russians at the end of WW2 and were handed over to us Brits when Berlin was cut into four sectors. The Berlin Wall ran along the perimeter of the barracks so the nosey Russians set up OP's (Observation posts) to look in. I heard they got mooned at least once a day.
The Barracks were renamed Montgomery Barracks, after Field Marshal Bernard Law Montgomery.
In 1993 the barracks were handed over to the German Bundeswehr (German Army) and renamed Blücher Kaserne.

'I sure do Eddie. I often wake up from a nightmare, after reliving that day when the cook-house ran out of bacon.'

'There are still unanswered questions about that day,' Eddie replied, with a sorrowful look on his face.

'Stop taking the piss, you two,' I said

'Well, I'm sick of his moaning. Give me compo any day of the week.'

'*Mmmmhh* orange-lard-encrusted-sausages! I'd kill for one of them right now: cheese possessed and babies heads, Wocko said, licking his lips.

'And if we're lucky, we might bump into Wolfgang and his Schnellie wagon,' Eddie added.

'Don't you mean he'll bump into us,' Wocko laughed.

'What's the betting he's sitting out there right now, ready to go, bratty's sizzling away, while he studies his fabloned map of the training area, with all our units, movements and red areas china graphed on it,' Clarkey said.

'Who is Wolfgang?' I asked.

'Who's Wolfgang? Wolfgang is a fucking legend.' Eddie sniffs the air. 'I can smell them now, *curried brat wurst mit pommes bitter.*'

'What's Eddie on about?' I asked, looking puzzled.

'God knows. I think he's trying to speak German,' Doubles replied.

'Wolfgang drives the local snack wagon around the training area. The man's, got godlike powers. It's amazing what that man can do with a dead horse and a few bags of old potatoes,' Eddie said.

'There is also a rumour, I don't know if this is true, that Neil Armstrong's famous *one small step* speech was interrupted by the sound of Wolfgang's vehicle horn sounding,' Clarkey added

'I heard that too Clarkey. I reckon he would open a snack wagon at the Everest base camp, and make runs to the summit, if there were enough climbers up there,' Wocko laughed.

'Alright, alright, you've made your point. If he's that good where is he now, to rescue us from this shite?' Doubles said, pushing his plate away.

'I know, why don't we all sneak out of camp and raid the nearest supermarket,' Wocko suggested.

'Wocko, do you hold your farts in?' Eddie asked.

'Sometimes I do, why?'

'Well, don't. They travel up your spine and into your brain. That's where shitty ideas come from. We're fucking miles and miles away from the nearest shop, never mind a supermarket.'

'Ok, ok. Keep your shirt on. It was only an idea,' Wocko said.

'I've got a Mars bar back in my tent. I'm open to offers.' Doubles piped up.

'Shut up, Doubles!' Eddie shouted at him.

The next few days became tedious, waiting for the exercise to start. There was nothing to do, unless you landed a guard duty or you were put on fatigues. We just prepared our kit, played cards for money or cigarettes, drank cheap beer and slept.

Being posted to Germany did have its perks though, even if it was only for 6 weeks. With the tax, free booze, fags, King Edward cigars, and other stuff. They even paid us overseas allowance. With not paying for food and accommodation, it meant a bumper, credits pay out when it came to summer leave.

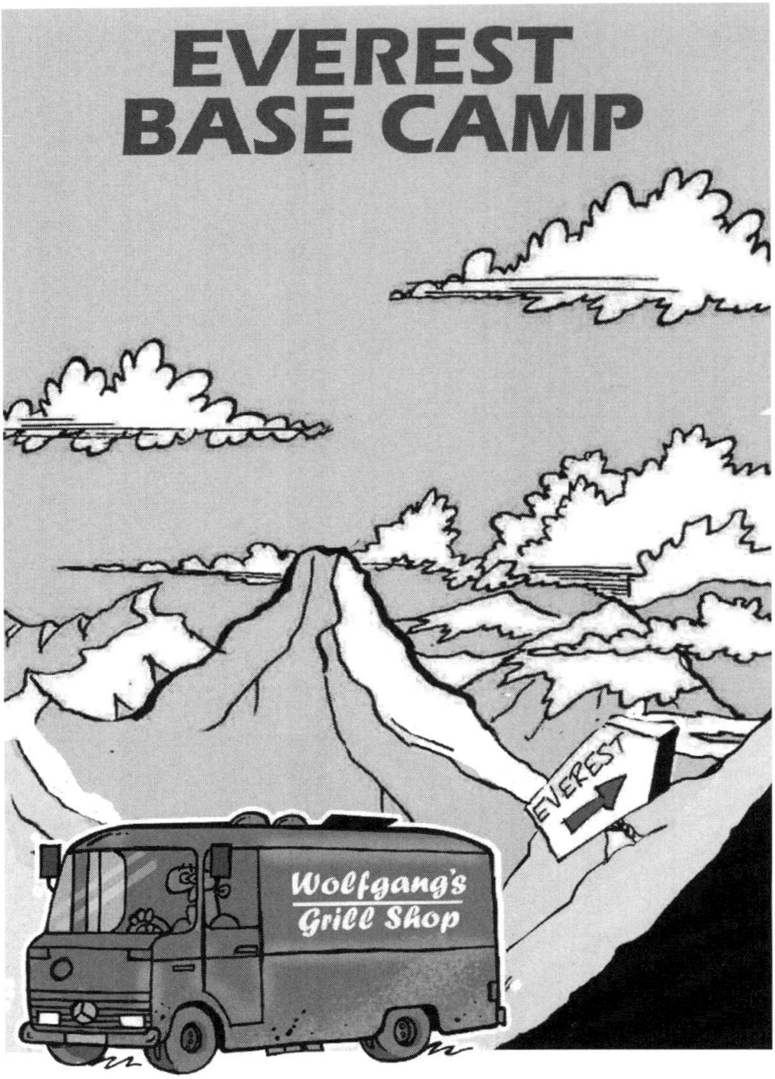
EVEREST
BASE CAMP
EVEREST
Wolfgang's
Grill Shop

> **Fact**
>
> In the 60's Rheinsehlen Camp had a camp switch board which still had eagle/swastika markings on it.

Punch-it

When the troops get bored they start to mess around, every platoon had their jokers, but sometimes things got out of hand.

To break the boredom, we played a game called PUNCH-IT. It involved placing a stick upright in the ground, then we'd all go off and find a small stone. The rules were simple, we'd all take turns in throwing our stones at the stick from about 10 yards away. The furthest one away from the stick got punched in the upper arm area by the nearest. It was really, funny to watch, unless you were the victim. Some 9 stone, weakling standing there, eyes shut, bracing himself, waiting for the impact of a punch thrown by some 17 stone beast.

It was probably the stupidest game ever, especially when the victim ended up with a broken arm, which happened on a few occasions. The game was later banned, which made it even more popular. I wonder if this game was played in other units. I'm sure it was, along with other dumb, bored on exercise games that were much worse.

Chapter 7

The next day, the boredom was broken by the PC's briefing about the forthcoming exercise, we were about to take part in. I can't recall the name of the exercise, as I was a 19, year old private. At that age, you didn't really give a shit what it was called. Added to that it was 40 years ago, and with age my memory is beginning to fail me. I don't even know what I had for breakfast this morning. But I know what it should have been called:
EXERCISE FREEZE 'UR FECKING NUTS OFF IN A GERMAN WOOD.
Most of what the PC said went through one ear and out the other, like the different stages of the exercise, what you could or couldn't do on the training area, and make sure you stayed in the red areas. Reinsehlen Camp was only part of a total of 4,600 hectares of red areas, named after the colour used on the maps in which military training was allowed all year. I think it was possible to enter the other areas, but you couldn't play war games in those areas.

Clive Ward

DAMAGE CONTROL

On some of the major NATO exercises in Germany, which I later took part in, nothing stopped the Allies from doing whatever they wanted, and if they were driving a 432 or a Tank even better.

Allied Tanks could suddenly turn off the road, and drive straight through fences, fields full of cabbage's, forest's and even get away with demolishing the odd building or two, causing thousands of Deutschmarks worth of damage, while the German Police could only stand there and watch. This was great for the local farmer or land owner, though, who then put a claim in, by filling out a compensation request form, given out by damage control officers, who were always close by, driving around in their little ferret cars.

'Eh mister tank commander, please knock down my rotten old barn, so I can get a new one for free! Oh, and here's 50 marks, slip that in your back pocket.' I have no doubt that happened more than once, allegedly.

On Soltau-Lüneburg it was slightly different, because it was an actual training area. There were rules that banned mock combat in the immediate surroundings of farms and villages, but the rules were often ignored, squaddies are *squaddies* after all. I suppose the rules were hard to enforce on 345 square kilometres of training area.

SOXMIS

We were introduced to the Soviet Exercise Mission cards, SOXMIS, in Soltau for the first time. SOXMIS were a small group of Soviet observers or 'authorized' spies who were allowed to roam around Western Germany's military zones, throughout the Cold War. Their cars were easily recognisable by special license plates with a large black number and a red Soviet flag on a yellow background.
Every NATO soldier was issued with, and had to carry, a SOXMIS Card, with details, on how to recognize the observers. The British Commanders'-in-Chief Mission to the Soviet Forces in Germany, BRIXMIS, was the British equivalent issued to the Soviet military. The reason for SOXMIS and BRIXMIS was to instil trust between the occupying powers in East and West Germany, but we all knew they were

there to report on each other's military capability. Only in the Cold war!

If we did spot one of these legal spies, we had to report them by phoning the number given on the card. The SOXMIS card was revised all the time and they were issued in all the languages of the NATO troops stationed in Germany.

I don't think we would be likely to see one in the middle of the Soltau training area, though, unless they were selling bratwursts!

I can remember going home on leave with one of these SOXMIS cards in my wallet. I felt very important when, giving my mates a quick knowing glance, I dropped it accidently-on-purpose, while paying for something at the shop or down the local pub, hinting that I was a Soviet Spy. Civvies would believe anything.

R&R

The only interesting bit of the briefing was when it came to our few days of Rest & Recuperation leave, which we all received towards the end of our 6 weeks in Germany. We could either save our money and chill out in camp, or go on the two organised trips. The trips couldn't be more different. I remember one of the trips was to Bergen Belsen Concentration camp, a place I'll never forget. The other was a trip to Hamburg and that was a place I'll definitely, never forget! The world famous Reeperbahn, a street lined with restaurants, night clubs, discotheques and bars. For us squaddies the important bits were strip clubs, sex shops, brothels, a sex museum and similar businesses. A squaddies paradise! Unfortunately, before the beer, sex and all that, we had to do the hard bit, digging trenches, staging on, and wandering around Soltau training area, in and out of full NBC kit for the next 4 weeks. It was hard work most of the time, but very enjoyable some of the time. The thought of the arranged trip to the red light, district at the end of the rainbow, would keep our dicks and our morale up.

Clive Ward

1. Colchester High Street in the 1970's.
2. Elvis Presley plus sideburns.
3. Aerial photograph of Colchester Garrison.
4. Soltau Bahnhof
5. Tank tracks, Lüneburger Heide training Area.

Bumpers & Bed Blocks

SIGHTING PROCEDURE
WHAT INFORMATION CAN I GIVE THE SOXMIS SIGHTINGS DESK
5. As quickly as possible after the sighting pass as much of the following information as you can to HERFORD Mil 2222
   a. Time and Place of Sighting.
   b. Colour and Make of Vehicle.
   c. Licence Plate Number.
   d. Number of Occupants and Dress.
   e. Direction of Travel.
   f. What occupants were doing.
   g. Any points of interest, ie Radio aerials, cameras, etc.

WHAT IF I CAN'T CALL IMMEDIATELY?
6. Your report will ALWAYS be useful, even if for some reason you cannot pass it on to the sightings desk immediately. So Phone it in as soon as you can!

1.

BFG FORM 66

SOXMIS

35

THIS IS A TYPICAL SOXMIS NUMBER PLATE
REMEMBER:
The number will be different on each car.

SOVIET MILITARY MISSION - BAOR

If you see a SOXMIS vehicle, contact as quickly as possible:
HERFORD Mil 2222
If using a German Civil Phone, dial:
a. In HERFORD code 89 then 2222
b. Elsewhere Code 05221-89 then 2222

2.

ONLY €5

3.

Herforder Handbag
8x330ml

4.

Es lebe die Deutsche Demokratische Republik - unser sozialistisches V...

1. SOXMIS card. 2. Yellow handbag, still selling 40 years later.
3. Tin pisser. 4. The Threat -T72 tanks.

89

Skive to Survive

In the early hours of the next morning, while the sky was still black, we stood on parade outside our tent with all our gear packed into our large packs, ready for inspection.

'Empty that large pack, Edwards,' Sergeant Billings said, pointing to Eddie's kit.

All that fell out was a large roll of bubble wrap, a pair of long Johns, a few pairs of dogs and a well, used, porn magazine.

'Bubble wrap? What the hell is that doing in there, Edwards?'

'It's in case I get bored on exercise, Sarge. I can pop the bubbles.'

'*Bored*... what a load of bollocks! The reason it's in there is because you are a lazy bastard, who filled his large pack with air, making it much lighter, which will allow you to enjoy a pleasant stroll in the countryside with your pals.'

'Sorry Sarge.'

'Sorry? That's what's found between shit and syphilis in the dictionary! Get your arse over to the platoon radio op and collect two radio batteries. By the way, you can wrap them in *your bubble wrap* to protect them if you want.'

'Where is the platoon radio op, Sarge?' Eddie asked pushing his luck.

'He's over there, the one in fucking green. How the fuck do I know? Find him. Give me your sleeping bag, Day,' Billings said, turning his attention to Doris.

He took the proffered sleeping bag from Doris, then he proceeded to turn it inside out, a solitary leaf fell out on the floor.

'What the fuck is a forest doing in your sleeping bag Day? Sort it out.'

A short time later, we piled onto our transport and off we went. In the back of the wagon we all sat quietly wondering what the next few weeks had in store for us. Our journey was quite short. Twenty minutes later, we arrived at the start point in the middle of nowhere.

'Come on, hurry up… let's have you off the truck. This is not a dream gentleman! This is fucking happening,' Sergeant Billings shouted.

As soon as we got off the vehicles, we were tactical. The vehicles disappeared and utter fucking chaos began. There was no moon, it was pitch dark, just the occasional flash of the Platoon Commander's torch, as he studied his map, pretending he knew where he was going. I hated tabbing, especially in the dark We stopped and started several times, then, suddenly without warning, we'd all concertina into each other.

The Equipment

They moan about the equipment today, but in the 70's, a lot of the kit we had to put up with was rubbish. And there was no writing off to the newspapers to complain about it. Back then you just got on with the job. It's what we had, but it never affected your ability to get the job done.

Tin Pisser

I always remember the tin helmets. They all had a two, inch rivet inside, which was designed to secure the inner lining (spider). More like designed to drill into the top of our fucking head, if the helmet inner was fucked or not fitted correctly or when we were hit on the head by our Platoon Sergeant, after being caught gonking on stag!

Water Proof

Then there was our waterproof, which we weren't allowed to wear on night patrol, because of the rustling noise it made. So, some of us wore them under our combat jackets. That had one major drawback, everything outside the waterproof got soaked by rain and everything under the waterproof got saturated with sweat.

Water Bottle Pouch

When our water bottle pouch got wet, we wouldn't dare take out our water bottle for a quick wet, because there was no fucking way it would go back in our now shrunken pouch, especially with the black mug attached.

Green Gloves

The woolly green gloves for the use of! Were you one of those who cut the fingers off? Did anyone ever have a pair that fitted them? Useless when wet and a pain in the arse when we found out we had two left handed gloves, for some strange reason we couldn't explain. Everyone in our platoon had left handed gloves. I'm sure that someone, somewhere has thousands of right handed gloved stashed away in the attic.

Large Pack

Why did they call it a *large pack?* It is a mystery to me because it wasn't large at all. We could hardly pack anything in it. If I remember correctly, there were straps all over the place for attaching sleeping bags, helmets & extra kit including shovels. With two large pouches at the sides to put your used smelly dogs and half opened bits of compo in. By the time, you'd finished attaching everything to it, you looked like a walking Christmas tree. Carry it for too long and you knew about it, the straps would cut into your shoulders. Thank God for the Bergen.

There were a few bits of kit that came in handy with their alternative uses. The poncho rolled up, made a great cushioned seat. The sleeping bag strapped on top of a large pack, made a perfect head rest, if we wanted to sneak a quick few minutes, zeds, whilst on a stop-start patrol. Eventually over the next few years, the kit started to improve, mainly because we purchased our own kit. The Bergen rucksack was very popular. Norwegian shirts improved our outfit. Likewise, the hi-lace Doc Martin's and thermals from M & S, although a pair of tights did the same job.

The Road to Nowhere

It seemed like we'd been tabbing for hours. The Platoon Commander was still having problems navigating.

'Do you want me to have a look at the map, sir?' Sergeant Billings asked.

'That's the second time you've asked me that Sergeant Billings. I'm quite capable of *wee*ding a bloody map you know,' the PC answered sounding flustered.

'Sorry sir, it's just that...'

'Come on sergeant, spit it out. What were you going to say?'

'That you took so long deciding whether to go left or right that I thought you were waiting for the UN to sort it out for you, sir.'

'Not funny Sergeant Billings,' he replied, handing Billings the map to study.

'Sir, why is there a wood to our left, but there isn't a wood on the map? Aren't we supposed to be sticking to the red areas?'

'That can't be *wi*ght. That wood shouldn't be there, according to the map,' the PC said looking confused.

'Look, sir, you're new to this game, so we expect you to fuck up from time to time, but don't abuse the privilege, okay?' Billings replied.

To be honest, I felt sorry for the PC, he was trying to do his best. The tracks marked on our issued *restricted* maps, were in reality, about, 300m wide and forked off all over the bloody place, due to the years of tracked vehicles wandering around Soltau lost. Someone in the ranks started to bleat, like a sheep.

Then came a few comments from the rear, 'right grid square... wrong planet...'
The usual, tell, tale sign the troops were getting pissed off and knew the, officer hadn't got a clue.

'Get on the *wa*dio and ask Z*ewo* whether we've got the wight gwid wefewence,' the PC instructed the guy who was carrying the radio.

'I beg your pardon, sir.'
'Give me the wuddy wadio.'

> ## The Larkspur
> The **Larkspur** system was replaced in 1980 by Clansman, which made everyone's life a lot simpler. Suddenly everyone was a radio op, even Wocko.

The PC began screaming down the Larkspur mike so loud that the receiving station HQ could hear him without a bloody radio. To make matters worse, so could the local taxi firm, ships in the channel, aeroplanes, the Kennedy Space centre and god knows who else who chatted away on the same frequency.

I never really had much time for the Larkspur radio. I think most operators were glad to see the back of them.

Because of frequency drift the operator had to do a radio check every 5 minutes or he had to re-tune. I can remember painstakingly forever retuning the bloody things and it wasn't easy, not everyone could do it.

The Larkspur radio did have advantages, though. The man pack radios used wax sealed batteries which meant once you had finished with them, they could be dumped. And dump them, we did, unless you shoved them in your mates, large pack without him knowing! Also, there was no battery charger to lump around.

While the PC struggled away on the radio, Sergeant Billings turned around to check on his men.

'Come on lads, close it up, you look like a sack of piss.'

Sack of piss... What the fuck is a sack of piss? Sergeant Billings would often come out with some classic one liner's, like the time he lost it on the range, and jumped down Doris's throat. "If you don't keep your weapon down the range, I'm going to slap you round the head like a ginger haired stepchild, "or, after witnessing an appalling lack of marksmanship, "look at that group, it looks like a mad woman's shite. What are you going to do when a fucking great Russian comes over the hill in front of you, with a big stick in one hand and a half-eaten baby in the other? Sort it out!'

The troops were now starting to get pissed off. We'd been carrying our kit for hours now, and the straps of our webbing and large packs were starting to cut into our skin which they often did.

'We're lost, aren't we Sarge,' Clarkey said.

'When I want your fucking opinion, I'll fucking give it to you Corporal Clarke.'

'I've had enough of this shit, whose turn is it to carry the Gimpie? I've been carrying it for ages. I'm knackered,' Doris moaned.

'Watkinson, take the Gimpie off Day,' Clarkey called out.

'Thank fuck for that... here cop that, Wocko,' Doris said, sounding relieved.

'There you go Doris.' Doris's GPMG was replaced with Wocko's 84mm anti-tank weapon, which was a lot heavier and more awkward to carry.

'Very funny Clarkey, I didn't know he had the 84mm,' Doris complained.

'That's what you get for whinging. Now, shut up and keep it down. We're supposed to be tactical.'

Unbeknown to Doris, he was also carrying two of Eddie's discarded radio batteries in his large pack. We didn't know it at the time, but the wood we were trying to find was only a few miles away. We must have tabbed around it about a dozen times. I think that's an experience every soldier worldwide has gone through more than once.

We finally arrived at our destination, after passing several other platoons, who looked equally lost. We lay in all round defence, until first light. At dawn, it was time to dig in.

We were to set up a defensive position along the edge of a wood, looking out over open ground. This was going to be our new home for the next few days, at least. It took us most of the day to dig our trenches. There was me and Eddie in one trench, Clarkey and Doubles, and Wocko and Doris in others. Doris was the lucky one sharing his trench, with an ex grave digger, Wocko was digging like a human JCB. Eddie and I had almost finished our trench, when Wocko and an angry Doris appeared.

'Finished already lads?' Eddie asked.

'There is no fucking way I'm spending the night in a trench with him. He fucking stinks,' Doris complained.

'Cool down Doris, it's only the first day. Give it a few days and you'll both smell the same,' Eddie said.

Wocko fired back. 'I'll stay in the trench on my own then. I practically dug the whole trench on my own anyway, while you just sat there you, lazy twat, writing to that slapper of yours. What's her name, Slacky Jackie?'

'Yeah, complete with its own shit pit. Yes, our trench is *en-suite*! By the way she's not a slapper, her name's Jacqueline. Speak about her like that again and I'll knock you out,' Doris retorted.

'A shit pit in a trench, that's a new one. Wocko you don't dig a shit pit in a trench, you go and dig a hole in the woods to shit, preferably down wind,' I advised.

'Too late! He's already christened it and it smells that bad it would scare a sewer rat away,' Doris said, as Wocko stood there smiling.

'For fuck's sake, I know people who set up charities for the likes of you Wocko,' Eddie said.

After a short negotiation, Doris paid Doubles to swap trenches, and the situation was resolved.

Before the light faded, Sergeant Billings and the PC came around to inspect the trenches and make sure we knew our arcs of fire. Our trench passed with flying colours. Then they visited Clarkey's trench. The PC and Sergeant Billings stood there looking confused.

'That's a well, constructed trench Corporal Clark, but there's only one problem,' said Sergeant Billings. 'You're facing the wrong fucking way.'

'You know, I thought there was something wrong, it just didn't feel right. So, the enemy's coming from that direction,' Clarkey said, pointing to his rear.

'Correct, God help us. Sort it out Corporal Clark.'

Then it was the turn of Wocko's trench. The first thing they noticed was a sign saying *shit pit this way, admission 1 DM,* with a black arrow pointing towards the rear of the trench. Doubles was on the make again.

'Dobson, why are you wearing your gas mask? Take it off,' the PC instructed.

'Yes, sir,' Doubles replied.

As they ventured closer to the trench, they picked up the smell. Within seconds they were both struggling to put on their gas masks.

'As you were Dobson, what on earth is that smell?' the PC asked.

'I covered it over with soil, but the smell doesn't seem to be going away,' Wocko said.

'Let me get this stwaight. You've dug a shit pit in the twench,' the PC replied.

'Watkinson, you've got an arse even a fucking dog wouldn't sniff. Dig it up and give it a proper burial in the woods,' Sergeant Billings added.

'But Sarge, I think it's a brilliant idea. What happens when you come under attack from the enemy, and you can't get out of your trench, for fear of getting shot or being hit with shrapnel?' Wocko tried to plead his case.

'He has got a point, Sergeant Billings,' the PC said.

'Sir with respect, I'd rather take my chances with bullet and shrapnel than stay in a trench with Watkinson, sir. You are a brave man, Dobson,' Sergeant Billings answered.

That night apart from sentry duty, we all slept soundly, but not Doris. Eddie told him there were still wild boar roaming around the woods in Germany. Doris took the bait, so much so that Eddie nearly gave him a heart attack when he crept up to him while he was on sentry and scared the shit out of him.

Chapter 8

Negligent Discharge

The next day we all sat patiently waiting for our enemy, the Orange force to arrive, hoping for things to kick off, but they didn't apart from when, at approximately 1200 hours, a shot was fired.

Eddie was cooking our compo dinner, while I watched to my front scanning for the enemy. I was growing bored, staring out over the open grassland in front of me.

'What made you join up Eddie?' I asked without looking away from the area in front of me.

'I got taken in by those posters, which read JOIN THE ARMY AND SEE THE WORLD. And I've been doing it a shovel at a time ever since! Can you see anything out there, Wardi?'

'Nah... I don't think we'll get any action for a few days yet. You know what these big exercises, are like,' I said playing with my safety catch. Out of boredom, I started playing war games pointing my weapon to my front. 'Enemy to my front, 3 o'clock, 200m......Watch my tracer!'

'You've got blank ammo, and you've got your BFA on, you thick twat,' Eddie said, laughing.

'What's for dinner?' I asked, annoyed at Eddie for squashing my war game dream.

'Powdered mashed potatoes, baby's head, and mixed veg.'

'Great I'm starving.'

Then a muffled BANG came, startling us both. As I lowered my SLR, it decided to fire a shot into the ground. 'What the fuck! I... Didn't do that, did I? Bollocks...'

'Whoops... you're in the shit now mate, negligent discharge. TUT..TUT.. That's at least a month's pay,' Eddie said.

'But I didn't do anything,' I replied, standing there like a lemon, wondering what the fuck had just happened.

'Of course you didn't. What the fuck do you think happened? It didn't fire its self, did it? How many times have I heard, that!'

I felt sick with worry and started to shake. I'd never had a negligent discharge before.

'Fuck me, you're as nervous as a white mouse in a tampon factory. Don't worry about it, leave it to me,' Eddie said.

Without a word of explanation, Eddie emptied the can of steak and kidney pudding all over me. My face and everywhere on the front of me, was covered with it.

'What did you do that for?' I asked.

'Keep your gob shut, trust me.'

A short distance away from our trench, the PC and Sergeant Billings, were also startled by the sound.

'That was a shot Sergeant Billings. Are we under attack?' the PC asked.

'I doubt it, sir. It was probably one of our own. Some idiot's probably had a negligent discharge.'

Sergeant Billings was on the war path, trying to find the culprit. It didn't take long before the PC and Sergeant Billings arrived at our trench.

'Right you two. What happened, who was it?' Sergeant Billings asked, narrowing his eyes.

'Who was what, Sarge?' Eddie answered.

'Who fired the shot?'

'What shot... oh that? That wasn't a shot. We just had a little accident, making our tea, didn't we Wardi? You see, our can of baby's head exploded. I forgot to pierce the can. Didn't I, silly me!' Eddie said, looking the picture of innocence.

'What a complete load of bollocks Edwards. That's the worst excuse in the history of excuses. That was a negligent discharge. Give me your weapons, I'll get to the bottom of this,' Sergeant Billings replied.

'Sergeant Billings stop this *wi*ght now. It's obvious to me this was an accident. Look at poor P*wi*vate Ward. It's a wonder he hasn't got first deg*wee* burns. Are you ok Ward?' The PC looked concerned.

'I'll live, sir, just minor burns. I think…' I answered, looking towards my feet. I knew if I looked the PC in the eye, he'd know I was lying.

An angry red faced Sergeant Billings and the PC wandered off back to their trench. The PC obviously wanted to draw a line under the incident.

'This goes no further Sergeant Billings. Any questions *w*aised on the *w*adio, deny everything.'

'Whatever, you say, sir.'

Eddie and I sat watching them, until they were out of sight. I heaved a sigh of relief, I'd managed to dodge a charge.

'You could have played on that Wardi. You could have had few days sick, back at camp, at the very least.'

'That would have been pushing it Eddie.'

Eddie then reached over and pulled a bit of steak and kidney pudding off my chin and tasted it, '*Mmmmm*, what a waste! It looks like cheese possessed and oatmeal for tea now.'

Yellow Handbags

That night and the following day, there was still no sign of the Orange forces. We knew they weren't that far away due to the rising dust clouds in the distance, and the roar from tank engines every now and then. On the third day, at last, we had activity. A little Mercedes blue van came bouncing up the track, bibbing his horn. It was the KGB's finest agent, Wolfgang.

Before he came to a stop, we all ran out and queued up like a load of kids in a sweet shop. We wanted our bratty's, pommes and one of those small bottles of Herforder Pils, sold in a yellow box with handles, hence the name of yellow handbags.
Sergeant Billings went ape shit, yelling at us to get back in our trenches. When he saw the PC at the

front getting served and trying to get information on the enemy's whereabouts, he changed his mind and took his place in the queue.

Along with our bratty and pommes, Wolfgang's was the best OGROUP (order group) you could attend. He could tell you everything, he was the best INTEL for miles around. He could even tell you when ENDEX was.

If there was a war, the enemy would find us straight away. All they would have to do is send out half a dozen blue vans. We would all come out of our trenches straight away, because we didn't like missing out on our curry würst and pommes.

Later on that afternoon the exercise kicked off. First came the clanging of mess tins and then the cry of GAS... GAS... GAS... the international alarm, indicating we were under chemical attack.

A decision, no doubt, made by some top brass at exercise control shouting GAS... GAS... GAS... down the radio. Then it appeared that this top brass must have been suffering from Alzheimer's, because for the rest of the exercise until ENDEX, our time was spent entirely in NBC suits.

We looked like tramps after a few days, never mind 3 weeks. I think the suits were only supposed to last 24 hours in battle. We didn't complain. Wearing our Noddy suits did have its advantages, but it also came with a few disadvantages.

The advantages of wearing the NBC suit were that on a cold day sat in your trench, it kept you warm and

Bumpers & Bed Blocks

snug. You could even grab some shut eye. With our S6 gas mask on, no one could tell we were sleeping, unless they got up close or we were snoring.
   The disadvantages of wearing them were; breathing out of your arse on a hot day running around the training area, playing war, trying not to drop dead from heat stroke. Taking the NBC suit out of our bum roll, or where ever we kept it, just before use, only to break out into a sneezing fit, after we realised that residual CS Gas was still present from the time we were practicing our NBC drills in the gas chamber back at Colchester.

If we ever came under a chemical attack at night, the enemy would know exactly where we were, due to the amount of coughing, sneezing and moaning we were doing. So, this is what all that NBC training, practicing drills, changing the canister, eating and drinking drills were for was it. Never understood that! Who the *fuck* would want to eat a cream *fucking* cracker while being pounded with lethal chemicals, let alone pull the respirator off in the middle of a nerve agent attack and reciting GOD SAVE THE *FUCKING* QUEEN and your name rank and number.
   The only time I ever put the gas mask to good use, was when I used it to scare the shit out of my roommates in the middle of the night, or when I got married. I used it to protect myself when it was my turn to change my baby's shitty arse. The best time to put the gas mask to the test was when the umpires arrived carrying their CS gas torches, waving them

around, trying to catch you off guard. As they were doing that, we were being attacked by pockets of the Orange forces on a reconnaissance mission, trying to test our strength.

'This could be our lucky day, Wardi. If we play our cards right, we could wangle a few day's as casualties,' Eddie said.

'If this is going to be another one of your madcap idea's Eddie, I don't want to know,' I answered. But I owed him a favour, so I was in.

The umpires always chose a handful of soldiers to become casualties, it made the exercise more realistic. Eddie and I planned it so that when the umpire passed us, we'd take our masks off, and with any luck we'd be in the back of a meat wagon taking it easy for a few days. The plan worked a treat. The PC and Sergeant Billings were furious.

'Where are you taking my men?' the PC demanded to know.

'Sorry sir' the umpire replied, 'these men are suffering from nerve agent poisoning.'

Eddie started coughing and rolling around on the ground like an octopus having an epileptic fit. While I tried to look like I was struggling to breathe, but my acting was hopeless.

'Fucking hell Edwards! Calm down, will you. What do you want an Oscar?' Sergeant Billings said, unimpressed by Eddie's acting skills.

'When will I get these men back?' the PC asked.

'Sorry I can't tell you that, sir, maybe in a few days.' Eddie took a pause from his acting session. 'A few days, but we've got nerve agent poisoning, that's bad, that's really bad. It'll be weeks until you see us again, surely,' Eddie said.

'Shut up Edwards. You're supposed to be dying, remember?' Sergeant Billings reminded him.

'They'll do their best to look after them, sir,' the umpire said, trying to reassure the PC.

The field ambulance soon arrived and they put us on stretchers, tagged us, and loaded us into the back and off we went, giving the PC and Sergeant Billings a sarcastic wave as we went.

'I can't believe our luck Wardi, proper food, clean sheets, here we come.'

But Eddie was wrong. The ambulance spent the rest of the day driving around the training area, picking up more mock casualties. Soon the ambulance was full.

'Any more bright idea's Eddie, I'm starving. I bet those bastards are tucking into our compo as we speak,' I said, before turning to the medic looking after us. 'What now?' I asked the medic.

'We're just waiting for one more casualty, and then we'll be heading back,' the medic replied.

'Back where, the field hospital?' Eddie said, with a smile.

'No, you're all going back to your companies,' the medic answered, grinning.

'Can't you take us back to the field hospital? Look our conditions are getting worse, we can pay,' Eddie pleaded.

The medic started to laugh. 'Sorry lads no can do, orders are orders.'

'Oh well, it was good while it lasted,' Eddie sighed.

A few hours later and we were back where we started, in our trench.

Top 20 Essential Pieces of Equipment to Take on Exercise

1. The laminated sick chit
2. Laminated Porn
3. Brew kit
4. Sense of humour
5. OXO cubes
6. Hip flask
7. Soft bog roll
8. JCB
9. A trench bitch
10. Lighter
11. Bacon
12. Beer
13. Spends
14. Woolly hat
15. Tabasco Sauce
16. Curry powder
17. Leave pass
18. Waterproof
19. Vaseline
20. Black bag

ENDEX

After another 2 weeks of creeping in and out of German woods, digging more shell scrapes and trenches, keeping our fingers crossed that a Chieftain tank didn't decide to roll over us we'd made it, ENDEX.

It didn't matter if we were freezing, piss wet through and starving, it was the best feeling in the world, climbing on the back of that Bedford, 4 ton truck. In seconds we were out like a light, deep sleeping all the way back to camp. It was good to get back and have a shower. After a few weeks on exercise, we had all started to smell like Wocko.

Bumpers & Bed Blocks

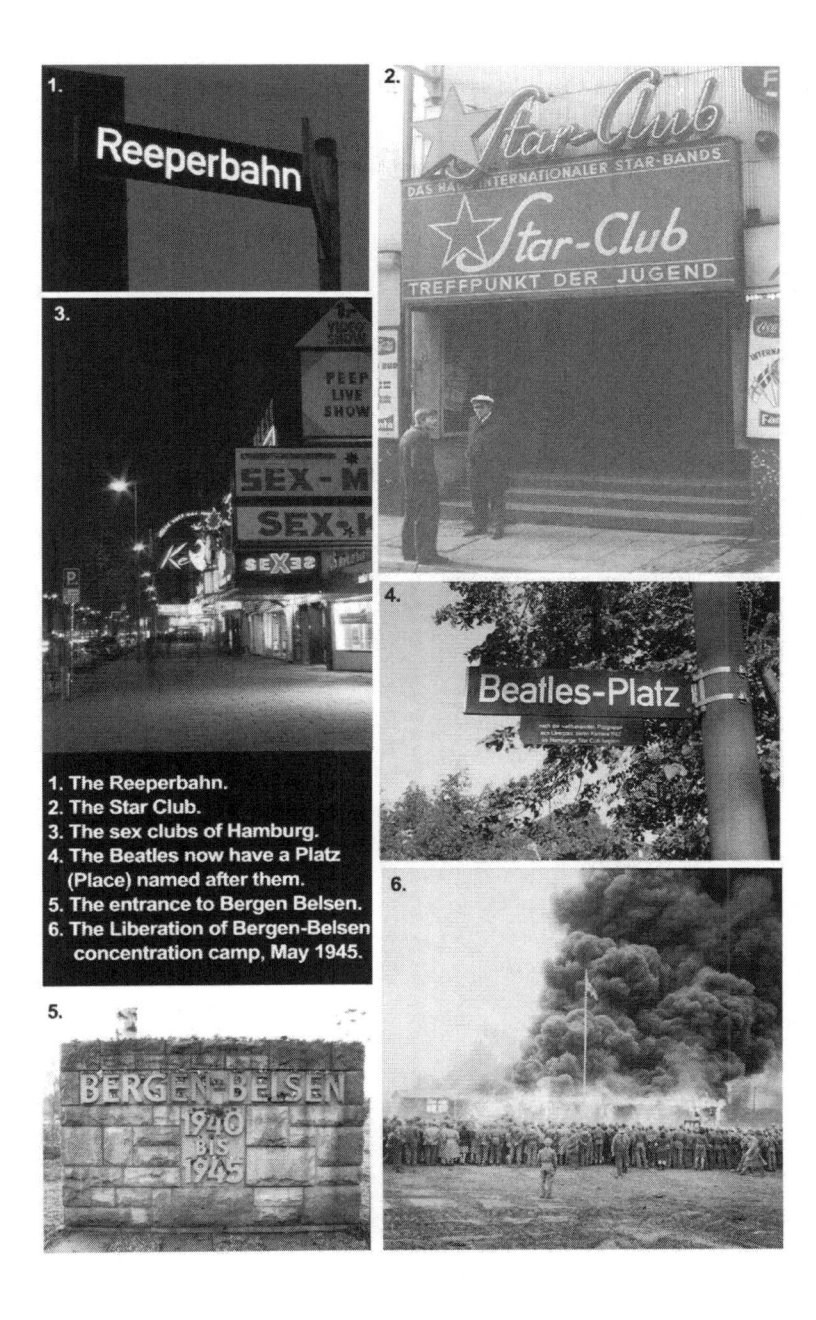

1. The Reeperbahn.
2. The Star Club.
3. The sex clubs of Hamburg.
4. The Beatles now have a Platz (Place) named after them.
5. The entrance to Bergen Belsen.
6. The Liberation of Bergen-Belsen concentration camp, May 1945.

115

Chapter 9

The Letter

That evening after de-gunge, we received our mail. Doris got the letter he'd been waiting for, a letter from his new girlfriend Jackie.

'I don't believe it, she's actually written to me,' Doris said smiling.

Doris never ever got proper mail. It was either a bill or a letter from a lonely hearts club, or a gay dating agency that we'd set up on his behalf.

'What you got there Doris, is it another lonely hearts letter?' Eddie teased.

'No, I've got a letter from Jackie. I knew she liked me.'

'Don't be taken in by her Doris, she doesn't like you.'

'Yes, she does.'

'No, she doesn't! She wouldn't have sent me those dirty photos for me to jerk off to,' Eddie replied, laughing.

'Fuck you Eddie.'

Doris started to shake as he opened his letter. Eddie continued to poke fun.

'Steady on Doris, that letter's not going spontaneously combust you know. Anyway, why would she write to you? You've got the personality of wallpaper.'

'What does it say Doris?' I asked.

'Yeah, come on Doris, spill the beans, out with it,' Clarkey said.

Doris lay there in silence, staring at his first ever letter from a female. But Doris had a big problem.

'You're wasting your time. Doris won't tell you what's in the letter, will you Doris? Eddie said.

'Leave him alone. It's private, isn't it Doris? It's between you and Slacky Jackie. I mean Jackie...' I replied, feeling sorry for Doris.

'Doris can't read, can you Doris?' Eddie answered.

'What? Is that right, can't you read Doris?' I asked, unable to believe it was true.

'I'll read it for you if you want,' Doubles offered, 'for £2. For another £2, I'll tell you what it says!'

'Wardi, will you read it for me?' Doris asked. 'Everyone else in here will take the piss.'

He handed me the letter and I started to read.

Dear Graham,

I'll tell you the truth. As I'm writing this letter, I'm pissed out of my face on vodka.

'Classy girl,' Eddie interjected.

To be honest, I haven't been in a relationship with anyone for a while, at least three weeks, that's why I know you are the one.

'Serious then,' Eddie added.

If you hear any rumours about me going out with two other blokes, ignore them. There are a lot of jealous bitches in Colchester, who don't like the fact I'm popular. All I did was accept a few drinks off the

blokes when I was downtown and they kindly escorted me home, but nothing happened, honest.
'Not that serious then.' Eddie was determined to make fun of the letter.
You're in my mind all the time, you make me so happy.
'She's definitely fallen for you Doris,' I said, before continuing to read.
Babe, I can't sleep because of you. Hurry home so we can get to know each other better. It's four am and I'm still awake.
'Poor girl,' Eddie just wouldn't give up.
Bloody taxi queue. The taxi rank outside the Grapes night club was massive. Anyway, I'm back home now, all tucked up in bed with Dillon keeping me warm.
'Who's Dillon?' I asked.
'It's her pet Rottweiler,' Doris answered, smiling.
By the way, let me know when you arrive back. I've told my mum, I've invited you back for tea. I hope that's ok? Anyway, I must sign off now.
Miss you.
Write back soon, all my love Jacqueline.
SWALK xxx
'What does *swalk* mean?' Wocko asked.
'*Sealed with a loving kiss* you, Muppet! Everybody in the entire world knows that,' I replied.
'Well, he didn't,' Eddie laughed.
'So, what do you put on your letters Wocko? AFRICA?' Eddie said.
'AFRICA? What does that mean?' Wocko looked totally baffled.

'AFTER FUCKING, RINSE IN CARBOLIC ACID,' Eddie answered, through his laughter.

'Well, I don't know what to say, being invited around to her mum and dad's house for tea. I reckon we'll soon be hearing wedding bells, Doris. What do you think Eddie?' I asked.

Suddenly, Eddie snatched the letter from my hand.

'Hold on there's more, *PS Get yourself checked out, I might have caught something,*' he joked.

'Don't be so disgusting, she wouldn't say that.' Doris looked upset.

'Calm down Doris, it was a joke,' Eddie replied.

Twenty-four hours later, we'd showered, covered ourselves with Brut or Old spice, changed into our civvies and boarded the army white buses. After travelling 80 kilometres, nearly the whole battalion descended on Hamburg's red light district.

Hamburg the Red-Light District

In the 1970's, Hamburg's St Pauli, where the Reeperbahn is located, was home to more than 1,000 prostitutes, more than enough for a battalion. Many plied their trade at the district's famous six-storey Eros center brothel, which then counted as one of the biggest in Europe. The brothel shut down in 1988, after the fear of the spread of Aids.

At that time, the red-light district was a den of drug dealers, users, pimps, whores and general iniquity! ... Yes, please bring it on, the perfect place for a night out for squaddies.

On the way there Eddie and Wocko started to fill my head with their past experiences when visiting the Reeperbahn, and the red light districts of Berlin. I was still only 19. I didn't show it, but I looked on the trip with a sort of nervous excitement.

 'Stick with me Wardi, you'll be alright,' Eddie said, 'no fucker will take me for a mug. You can lose all your money in seconds if you don't know what you're doing in these places. It only takes 5 minutes, and you'll have100DM less in your pocket and its welcome to Germany.'

We got off the buses, walked up the hill and started to take in the delights of Hamburg's red light district, the Reeperbahn. From the start the place fascinated me, like it would anyone else experiencing it for the first time.

> **The Reeperbahn is named after the city's rope makers. Originally, Hamburg's rope makers had been located in the New Town quarter in the inner city, but following extensive building in the area, it became overcrowded. The rope makers then moved outside the city to a country road, which later took on the street name 'Reperbahn,' which when translated is ropewalk.**

A lot of the lads piled into the live sex shows. They paid a small fortune for their drink and that entitled them to sit and watch a live show. It could be a girl on the stage with a snake, a stripper, a sex scene. Those shows found every way possible to titillate the audience. Some of the lads were even invited up on the stage to join in with the fun, if they were lucky, brave, or stupid enough. Usually they ended up making complete twats of themselves, trying to be the next Ron Jeremy porn star. Of course the girls would be all over them making out they were enjoying it too. But they'd done this routine millions of times. An industrial steam driven hammer wouldn't turn these girls on, it was just work. Thank God there were no camera phones in those days.

After visiting a few peep shows, we wandered past the many windows with prostitutes on display sitting under red neon lights. Some of the girls tried their hardest to attract us inside and take our money. Others just stared vacantly, expressionless. There was every nationality you could think of, any size or shape, from African 400-pounders, to tiny Asians or silicone blondes. There were all sorts, we could take our pick. The spectacle was sad, really.

Walking through the district, we saw all kinds of individuals. Soldiers, sailors, dirty old men, couples just taking a stroll, drunk couples, drunk revellers talking loudly, getting into fistfights and sexualising just about everything in sight... And there was always a policeman around the next corner.

> **Did you know?**
>
> In the early 1960s, The Beatles, played in several clubs around the Reeperbahn.

It was while we were walking past the windows, that we lost Doubles and Doris. Having a new girlfriend, Doris was on his best behaviour. Before we left camp, he gave Doubles his wallet for safe keeping, and told him not to give him any money to go with any of the whores under any circumstances. The rest of us, me Eddie, Wocko and Clarkey had other ideas.

'Where did Doubles and Doris get to?' I asked, realising they were missing.

'God knows. Don't worry, there'll be around here somewhere. If not we'll see them when we get back on the bus anyway,' Wocko replied.

'I don't want to hang around with those two anyway. Doris is love struck and Doubles is that tight, he's probably asking the girl to pay him for sex,' Clarkey joked.

'I know another area at the top of the hill, with some great bars, where we won't get ripped off. We need to get away from here, there's too many pissed up squaddies for my liking,' Eddie said.

We had to be back on the buses by midnight. Time was running out, we only had a few hours left. We headed for the first bar we saw. We found a quiet bar that looked ok. A huge bouncer stood at the entrance trying his best to entice us in.

'Gentlemen, gentlemen don't walk by. You like what you see? Come on in guys, just have one drink, you won't be disappointed,' he said, smiling at us.

We all peeped inside. The place was dark, but we could see a few scantily clad, nice looking girls mooching around. And best of all no sign of any troops. We all decided to go for it, and in we went.

In Hamburg, as in most German cities and cities across the world, there are walk-in brothels of varying repute. If people choose to enter them, they just need to keep switched on. Some of these bars will try to catch people out in the oldest scam trick in the book. There are people that still fall for it, and there always will be. As long as there are pissed up, gullible squaddies around and their like, there'll always be scammers. That day we were the victims, well nearly.

We knew the first drink was always expensive in these places, but when we got the drinks menu they weren't that bad, or so we thought. The plan was to buy our drinks and make them last us, as long, as we could.

The Scam

This is how the scam works. The guy would be sitting there in a dark corner or booth, when two or three sexy women would appear and cuddle up to him, then start touching him up, getting him all excited. Suddenly he thinks 'I'm in here.' No, you're not by the way... Then they'll get him to order them and himself more drinks. Their drink is usually a 20DM bottle of champagne, champagne my arse, it's more likely cheap sparkling wine, crap that they couldn't get pissed on. They drank that so that they stayed sober enough to fleece his wallet. After a few more drinks, the bill starts to mount up and he then realises the furthest he's going to get with these girls, is a quick grope, if he's lucky. Then the penny finally drops. He's getting scammed. Now he needs to get the fuck out of there. That's when he receives the drinks bill, and nearly falls off his chair.

This is the moment he realises he's made a big mistake, now he won't be allowed to leave unless he pays the bill, either with cash or by credit card. If he refuses, they'll threaten him, and if that doesn't work they will call the police. Then the police show up and point out to him that he is attempting to leave without paying. He knew the price of the drinks when he walked in they'll say. The actual drinks menu was outside, on the door. In Germany by law, you have to display the drinks menu outside the venue. So, people knew what they were going to pay before they entered. The over friendly bouncer stood in front of it, but the customer was too busy looking at the girls inside to worry about that.

Once inside the building, the drinks menu they were given to order the drinks from, had prices that were a lot cheaper. But now that cheaper drinks menu has mysteriously disappeared, leaving just one menu, the one on the door. That 20DM bottle of champagne they bought for the girl sitting on their lap is now 50DM. Technically, they have him by the bollocks. The bouncer, bartender and the girls, and I bet, even some of the police back then, were all working together. They were all after a share of your money.

You've Pulled

In our case, it was slightly different. We made our way to the rear of the bar, it was really dark, but we thought nothing of it. We ordered our drinks from the menu. We noticed all the drinks had stupid, bizarre names. We sat waiting patiently for the women to arrive. Fifteen minutes had passed. We started to

wonder what was happening.
'Where are all the women Eddie?'
'Patience, Wocko, patience.'
Having nearly finished our drinks, we contemplated leaving, when suddenly out of the darkness, a girl appeared. She walked over and sat on my lap.
We started to talk a bit, frolic a little, giggle a bit and drink.
'Fuck me Wardi, it looks like you've pulled,' Wocko said.
I couldn't believe it, it was still a little dark, but she looked ok to me. Things were starting to liven up when another girl arrived. After suffering the ultimate embarrassment of being turned down a number of times by the window girls earlier, even Wocko pulled. They got us to order more drinks, including their bottle of lemonade piss, pretending to be champers, but we weren't bothered. We were loving the attention. Then it was Eddie's turn. The girls were all over us. The worrying thing was, they were starting to get uglier. The only one left without a girl was poor Clarkey, who sat there like a naughty child looking well pissed off.
'What about me, am I fucking Frankenstein, or something?' he moaned.
'Let's face it, you're an ugly cunt Clarkey,' Eddie said.
'Fuck off Edwards, you twat!'
Then it happened. Out came a right monster, a thing with a face that could sink a ship. She was wearing a Basque, fishnet stockings and suspenders. She made a beeline for Clarkey and plonked herself down

on his knee.

'Fuck me Clarkey,' Wocko joked, 'the eagle has landed.'

'Anybody seen that film Frankenstein's Bride,' Eddie laughed.

She also had an Adam's apple the size of a golf ball and that wasn't the only thing sticking out! Without any warning, Clarkey decided to push his admirer in the face and onto the floor.

'They're blokes, you, Muppets!' Clarkey cried, jumping to his feet.

He was right. We'd been chatted up by a bunch of lady boys. Now the other lady boys started to kick off. The whole place erupted. We had to fight our way out of there, past two big bouncers. We ran like hell all the way back to the waiting white buses. There were police everywhere after that, we thought ourselves lucky we'd escaped with just a few minor cuts and bruises, and some damaged pride. We never did mention it to the other lads for obvious reasons.

We should have realised the place was a transvestite club. How could we have missed the warning signs? They were there alright, some of them had voices deeper than a lumberjack with a sore throat, and one could only marvel at the size of their big shovel like hands trying to fondle your wedding tackle.

Cock a Lada

But the biggest give away was when we ordered our first drinks. We all ordered a bizarrely named beverage called "Cock a Lada." I think it must have been that, I bet it was that, that misguided us. It must have been some sort of drug.

Man down

It was when we got back to the bus, and Sergeant Billings was doing the roll call, we found out we were a man down. Lover boy Doris had gone missing.

'Doubles, where's Doris? I heard he was with you,' Sergeant Billings said.

'I left him in the Reeperbahn, Sergeant. He was out of his tree. Earlier, he gave me his wallet and told me not to give him any money out of it. But he suddenly changed his mind after spotting this girl sitting in one of the windows. She was the spitting image of his new girlfriend. He then demanded his wallet back. He got really mad when I refused to give it him,' Doubles replied.

'You didn't give it to him, did you?' Sergeant Billings asked.

'I had no choice. He just went on and on and started to attract attention. He wouldn't shut up, so I gave him 100DM. Then he just disappeared inside. I waited and waited, but the local coppers told me to stop loitering and moved me on, so I came back.'

I spotted the PC approaching the bus. He'd obviously realised there was a problem, having seen Sergeant Billings glowering at Doubles.

'What is it Sergeant Billings?' he asked, as he got on the bus.

'Man down, sir. Day has gone missing.'

'But the buses are leaving in 10 minutes.'

'He knows the bus leaves at midnight. We'll just have to leave him here, sir. He can make his own way back to camp, and answer for it tomorrow, sir.'

'Leave him here, Sergeant Billings? We never leave a man behind, anything could have happened to him. We need to send out a search party... this is a man down situation.'

'Sir with respect, this is hardly the streets of Belfast, this is the red light district. Knowing Day, he's probably tied to a bed in one of them brothels being shagged senseless by some whore.'

Eddie decided to butt in. 'Then some fat guy dressed as Batman, jumps out of the wardrobe and takes over, poor Doris.' Everyone started to laugh.

'Not funny Edwards,' Sergeant Billings said, with a stern look on his face.

'For all we know Edwards could be *wight*. That's why we should get out there and *wescue* him at once.' The PC sounded worried.

Doris chose that moment to stagger onto the bus, with the biggest black eye you've ever seen.

'Shit! What happened to you?' I said, staring at Doris' eye.

'You idiot Doubles! I've just been chased by half the whores in Hamburg,' Doris complained.

'Thank God you're back Day! We were about to send out a search party,' the PC informed him.

Sergeant Billings and the PC walked to the front of the bus and sat down, and instructed the driver to head back to camp.

'What happened?' Eddie asked.

'When I got inside, I thought fuck it. I'll go for it and have two girls at 50DM a time.'

'You had a twosome, you lucky bastard. Was it good?' Wocko said.

'It was amazing, the best shag I've ever had.'

'Don't you mean the only shag you've ever had?'

'Shut up Eddie, let him tell his story,' Wocko replied.

'And then it came to paying them,' Doris said, turning to Doubles with an angry face. 'Doubles you idiot, you gave me a 10DM bill not 100DM. Within seconds they were at least about to string me up, when I told them I couldn't pay. I had no choice. I got the fuck out of there. I've just been chased around most of fucking Hamburg, by a bunch of angry whores and pimps. My eye's killing me. One of the girls hit me with a spanking paddle.'

Doubles shrugged his shoulders, 'sorry my mistake.'

'So, what happened to you lot?' Doris asked, looking directly at Eddie.

'Oh, we just went for a quickie, a few drinks and headed back to the bus. Didn't we, lads?' Eddie answered.

There were lots of stories that night. To be honest, I think a lot of the lads just wanted to say, when they got back to camp, that they had the best time. Nearly everyone said they'd been with a whore. It was sort of a badge of honour. In reality, only a few did the deed, most of them hadn't. They'd gone into some live show and had been fleeced more like, or opted to knock one out in the wank closets or video booths that were spread around the district. They were cheaper and there was less chance of their cock dropping off.

Spare a thought for the lad who got more excitement than he bargained for in one of the sex shops. He dozed off in a video booth, got locked in overnight and was mistaken for a burglar by police, as he tried to get out. I can't remember what happened to him.

We arrived back at camp in the early morning. Our visit to Germany was nearly over.

We heard when we got back to camp that a couple of the lads had got a young soldier really pissed. They thought it would be a good idea to sell him to a couple of gays for 200DM. They got worried though, when he didn't turn up for the bus on time. When he did eventually return, he had the biggest smile on his face, they looked on in confusion.

Those were the days. The old pimps of the red, light district would tell anyone prepared to listen, that today the place has become too commercial, it isn't the same. It's now over-run by young men on stag nights. The peep shows have been replaced by run-of-the-mill discos, blasting out loud shite music. The sex industry has been replaced pretty much wholesale, by the tourist industry. Is that a good thing? I bet most squaddies would say no.

Chapter 10

On my last day in Germany we visited The Bergen Belsen Memorial site. Back then this was the first ever permanent exhibit anywhere in Germany on the topic of Nazi war crimes. With only a caretaker as permanent staff, the memorial events were only organized by the survivors themselves.

On entering the site I noted the absence of bird song. A sobering and lifeless place, it was like things didn't want to be there. Stone markers merely stating *here lay 5,000 dead. April 1945.* The weather that day was dull and grey, matching the surroundings.

I read somewhere that the reason there are no birds near the mass graves was the high alkaline content levels in the soil, caused by the quick lime used to cover the corpses. Worms and other insects cannot live in this environment, making it hard for the birds to feed.

Bergen-Belsen or Belsen, was a Nazi concentration camp, originally established as a prisoner of war camp. In 1943, parts of it became a concentration camp. The number of people killed there, is still to this day unknown, but it is thought to be more than 50,000 in the concentration camp alone.

The camp was liberated by the British 11th Armoured Division on April 15, 1945. The soldiers discovered around 60,000 prisoners inside, most of them half-starved and seriously ill, and another 13,000 corpses lying around the camp unburied.

After liberation 13,994 people died, in spite of massive efforts to help the survivors with food and medical treatment. The British comedian Michael Bentine, took part in the liberation of the camp. There is also a Memorial for Margot and Anne Frank at the former Bergen-Belsen site.

Following financial help from the Federal Government, the memorial was redesigned and opened to the public in 2007.

End of Era

After the Berlin Wall fell in 1990, we stopped protecting the Fatherland from the impending arrival of the Red army. The British Military started to wind down training at Soltau-Lüneburg during the region's peak tourist season, the period when the heather blooms.

On 17 October 1991, the German Minister of Defence and the British Secretary of Defence, signed an agreement to end training in the Soltau-Lüneburg area by 1994. The heather had won the day. The training finally stopped on 1 July 1994 and the British forces left along with Wolfgang, who went on to pastures new.

Exercise Womble 2001

Over the years, the training activities had caused a large amount of damage to the environment, especially in the red areas. The camp was searched for areas of contamination and in two places high readings of chemical pollution were discovered. Plus, thousands of tons of Wolfgang's cooking oil, I have no doubt. It began the biggest area cleaning exercise of all time. The British government spent around 10.2 million DM in 2001 to restore the red areas.

What used to be Rheinsehlen camp is now a hotel/outdoor complex. Gone are the Nissan hut accommodations, they've all been pulled down, and there's no sign of the hard standing buildings, it's all overgrown.

What a place, all those memories. That's why I wrote them down, we can't let them be forgotten. Some of the stories might have been exaggerated along the way, but most of them are just as I remember them.

I returned to Germany in 1980 with my battalion. We were to spend 5 years in Hemer/ Iserlohn as mechanised battalion, but that's another story.

Happy Families

Arriving back in the UK, once all our admin was done, we had the rest of the day off to do what we wanted. Doris' first port of call was to visit the pox doctor to get treatment for something he had caught while visiting Hamburg, along with half a dozen other lads. It was confirmed he'd caught the clap, much to the amusement of Sergeant Billings.

That night most of us headed downtown for a drink. But Doris, now dosed up with medication for his rotting John Thomas, was off to meet up with Slacky Jackie and her parents. Dressed in his best civvy clothes, it was obvious he was nervous by the way he kept checking his appearance in the mirror.

'Don't you bastards say anything about me catching a dose to Jackie,' Doris said.

'Bloody hell Doris, what do you take us for? That's a bit below the belt!' Eddie replied, with a serious look on his face.

'Well, I'm off lads,' Doris added, as he took a last look in the mirror.

'Good luck with the future in-laws Doris. I hope you make a good impression,' Wocko called after him.

After Doris left the room, Eddie and the others started to laugh. Some of them were doubled over. I didn't have a clue what they were laughing at.

'What's so funny Eddie, what are you laughing at?' I asked.

'I'd love to be a fly on the wall when he meets Jackie's dad, and finds out it's none other than our very own Sergeant Billings.

Bumpers & Bed Blocks

Glossary (Civvies and Walt's only)

AWOL/Absent without leave

Babies heads/ Steak & Kidney puddings

Barrack room/Accommodation

Beasted/Pushed to the limit

Bed Blocks/ Sheets and blankets folded together to form a block, with pillows on top.

Bed space/ The area around your bed

BFA/Blank firing attachment

Brasso/Metal polish

Bulling Boots/Polishing boots to a high sheen like glass

Bumper/Floor polisher

Cam cream/Camouflage cream

Charge/On report

Cheese possessed/ Processed cheese

Compo/Composite rations

Cook House/Canteen

Diggers/Knife Fork and Spoon (KFS)

Dogs/Socks

Fatigues/Extra duties

Gob smacked/Surprised

Gonking/sleeping

GPMG/General Purpose Machine Gun

Locker/Wardrobe

Maggot/Sleeping bag

Naafi/Navy, Army, Air Force Institute Shop

NBC suit/ Nuclear, Biological, Chemical protective suit.

NCO/Non Commissioned Officer

Noddy suit/NBC suit

Non tac/Non tactical

PC/Platoon Commander

Pit/Bed

Quick wet/Cup of tea

Razzer/Regimental Sergeant Major/RSM

Rippers/Restriction of privileges

Room jobs/Cleaning duties

R & R/ Rest & recuperation leave

Scran/Food

Sergeant/Sergeant

Skiddies/Underpants

SLR/Self Loading Rife

SMG/Sub-Machine Gun

Squaddie/A soldier

Square/The parade square

Stag/Guard duty

Tabbing/Marching in full kit with weapons at a fast pace

Todger/Penis

Trench/Hole in the ground

Wagon/Military vehicle

Wank mag/Pornographic magazine

Wombling/Area cleaning

Clive Ward

Photographic Credits

Garrison Church, page 58, image 6.
Image available at; https://en.wikipedia.org/wiki/Colchester_Garrison

- Image Copyright Glyn Baker. This work is licensed under the Creative Commons Attribution-Share Alike 2.0 Generic Licence. To view a copy of this licence, visit http://creativecommons.org/licenses/by-sa/2.0/ or send a letter to Creative Commons, 171 Second Street, Suite 300, San Francisco, California, 94105, USA.

MCTC Colchester, page 59, image 1.
Image available at; http://www.geograph.org.uk/reuse.php?id=63934

- Image Copyright Glyn Baker. This work is licensed under the Creative Commons Attribution-Share Alike 2.0 Generic Licence. To view a copy of this licence, visit http://creativecommons.org/licenses/by-sa/2.0/ or send a letter to Creative Commons, 171 Second Street, Suite 300, San Francisco, California, 94105, USA.

Meanee Barracks, page 59, image 4.
Image available at; http://www.geograph.org.uk/photo/1459081

- Image Copyright Glyn Baker. This work is licensed under the Creative Commons Attribution-Share Alike 2.0 Generic Licence. To view a copy of this licence, visit http://creativecommons.org/licenses/by-sa/2.0/ or send a letter to Creative Commons, 171 Second Street, Suite 300, San Francisco, California, 94105, USA.

Elvis Presley, page 88, image 2.
Image available at;
https://commons.wikimedia.org/wiki/File:Elvis_Presley_Publicity_Photo_for_The_Trouble_with_Girls_1968.jpg
The image is in the public domain.

Bumpers & Bed Blocks

Colchester Garrison, page 88, image 3.
Image available at; http://www.geograph.org.uk/photo/2132450

- Image Copyright terry joyce. This work is licensed under the Creative Commons Attribution-Share Alike 2.0 Generic Licence. To view a copy of this licence, visit http://creativecommons.org/licenses/by-sa/2.0/ or send a letter to Creative Commons, 171 Second Street, Suite 300, San Francisco, California, 94105, USA.

Soltau Bahnhof, page 88, image 4.
Image available at; https://commons.wikimedia.org/wiki/File:Soltau_Bahnhof.jpg
Image is in the public domain.

Lűneberger Heide, page 88, image 5.
Image available at;
https://commons.wikimedia.org/wiki/File:L%C3%BCneburger_Heide_1960_003.jpg

- Image by Nikanos. This work is licensed under the Creative Commons Attribution- Share Alike 1.0 Licence. To view a copy of this licence, visit http://creativecommons.org/licenses/by-sa/2.0/ or send a letter to Creative Commons, 171 Second Street, Suite 300, San Francisco, California, 94105, USA.

The Threat T 72 Tanks, page 89, image 4.
Image available at;
https://commons.wikimedia.org/wiki/File:Bundesarchiv_Bild_183-1988-1007-008,_Berlin,_39._Jahrestag_DDR-Gr%C3%BCndung,_Parade.jpg

Attribution: Bundesarchiv, Bild 183-1988-1007-008. This work is licensed under the Creative Commons Attribution- Share Alike 3.0 Licence. To view a copy of this licence, visit http://creativecommons.org/licenses/by-sa/3.0/ or send a letter to Creative Commons, 171 Second Street, Suite 300, San Francisco, California, 94105, USA.

The Star Club, page 115, image 2.
Image available at;
https://commons.wikimedia.org/wiki/File:STAR-CLUB_Eingang_Hamburg_1968.jpg

- Image by ThomasFHH. This work is licensed under the Creative Commons Attribution- Share Alike 4.0 International Licence. To view a copy of this licence, visit http://creativecommons.org/licenses/by-sa/4.0/ or send a letter to Creative Commons, 171 Second Street, Suite 300, San Francisco, California, 94105, USA.

The Sex Clubs, page 115, image 3.
Image available at; https://simple.wikipedia.org/wiki/Reeperbahn

- Image by dannyone. This work is licensed under the Creative Commons Attribution- Share Alike 3.0 Licence. To view a copy of this licence, visit http://creativecommons.org/licenses/by-sa/3.0/ or send a letter to Creative Commons, 171 Second Street, Suite 300, San Francisco, California, 94105, USA.

Beatles Platz, page 115, image 4.
Image available at;
https://commons.wikimedia.org/wiki/File:Beatles_Platz_Hamburg.JPG

- Image by Heide-Daniel. This work is licensed under the Creative Commons Attribution- Share Alike 3.0 Unported Licence. To view a copy of this licence, visit http://creativecommons.org/licenses/by-sa/3.0/ or send a letter to Creative Commons, 171 Second Street, Suite 300, San Francisco, California, 94105, USA.

Bergen-Belsen, page 115, image 5.
Image available at;
https://commons.wikimedia.org/wiki/File:Bergen-belsen.jpg

- Image by Arne List. This work is licensed under the Creative Commons Attribution- Share Alike 3.0 Unported Licence. To view a copy of this licence, visit http://creativecommons.org/licenses/by-sa/3.0/ or send a letter to Creative Commons, 171 Second Street, Suite 300, San Francisco, California, 94105, USA.

Liberation of Belsen, page 115, image 6.
Image available at;
https://commons.wikimedia.org/wiki/File:The_Liberation_of_Bergen-belsen_Concentration_Camp,_April_1945_BU4242.jpg

Image is in the public domain.

Bumpers & Bed Blocks

Clive Ward

Printed in Great Britain
by Amazon